Straight Talk:

Unintended Consequences

By

Rick Montana

Printed by CreateSpace

ISBN: 978-1508863014

No one was more surprised than Rick Montana when a UFO swooped down and abducted him, motorcycle and all. The aliens gave him a series of lectures on their interaction with humans over the centuries. He learned the aliens have been conducting experiments on the inhabitants of several planets, including Earth. They pick a life form on each planet and manipulate their brains from time to time and then wait a few years to judge the results. Often there are unintended consequences. It is time to make a decision about whether the aliens destroy mankind and start over or give us more time to develop into a worthy species. After hearing the aliens describe the mess humans have made over the years, it doesn't look good for the home team.

CHAPTER ONE

Abduction

I have always been interested in the subject of people being abducted by aliens. During work on a low budget movie in Los Angeles, I actually spoke at length with a person who is famous for being one of the most "alien abducted" people in America. He claims to have been abducted by aliens, starting at age five, and continuing throughout his life. I really thought I knew what to expect if it ever happened to me. Boy was I wrong! What self described alien abductee Jesse Long, Jr. described was nothing like what I experienced during my stay with the aliens.

It all started late one night when I was out for a ride on my Harley. If you wait until late at night, after it gets a little cooler, there aren't as many bugs around. Now if you've ever rode a motorcycle, you know what I'm talking about. Anyway, there I was cruisin' along, enjoying the cool breeze and the full moon that seemed to light up the whole scene. You could almost drive without headlights, it was so bright. I was more or less lost in thought as I rode through the night while my mind drifted from topic to topic. At this point, things got a little strange.

Have you ever had the feeling that someone is behind you, yet when you turn to look, no one is there? Well, I certainly had that feeling. With my mind wandering and my Harley cruising along at a smooth sixty-five miles per hour, I suddenly realized that I was in a place I didn't recognize. There was a smooth looking side road up ahead with a sign that said "Mississippi River 1 mile." With very little thought, I took that turn and ended up in outer space!

What happened after I took that turn is a little foggy. I kind of remember my motor going dead and I coasted to a stop on the side of the loneliest looking road you ever saw. Nothing was moving anywhere and it was so quiet that you could hear the metal of my engine popping as it cooled down. My Harley is new enough that it doesn't even have a kick starter on it. Either the electric start works or you push it. I picked a totally different option. I chose to just sit there awhile, enjoying the night, all the time hoping that eventually it would heal itself and crank again. As I sat there, the hair on my neck began to stand up and I felt a little peculiar. I looked up and there above me was this huge saucer shaped craft. It just kind of appeared. No noise, no nothing. Suddenly I was surrounded by the brightest light I ever saw. The next thing I know, I'm sitting on my Harley inside that thing!

At first I just sat there, kind of stunned. There was plenty of room and no one was around, so I finally got off the bike and started looking around. There was not much to see as this appeared to be some kind of storage area with no way in or out. Just when I was about to give up, a door appeared in the otherwise smooth wall. Four of the strangest looking individuals I have ever seen walked in. They looked a lot like the aliens described in stories and movies. They had large heads on willowy bodies with long fingers on their hands. Their eyes seemed very large for their face and seemed to look

2

right through you. Their mouths were small as were their ears which lay flat against their head. They stood about five feet tall, except for one who was about five foot six. He was clearly the leader. They wore very tight fitting uniforms which almost seemed like a second skin. I don't know about you, but I was very impressed.

You would probably be surprised to know that instead of being afraid, I was thinking about how much like Hollywood aliens, these aliens looked. How did so many people get it right? Had thousands of people already seen these guys and no one would believe them? Like a light coming on, I realized this must be so. My next thoughts were "why me". What could I have ever done to attract the attention of these aliens? Was I just in the wrong place at the wrong time or was there more to it. The answer to that question wasn't long in coming.

CHAPTER TWO

Why Me?

The aliens stood in a semi circle around me and my Harley. They were looking at me as if I were a display in a museum. They seemed to be taking in every detail. A couple of them seemed just as fascinated by my motorcycle. They kept changing position and looking so much alike, that it wasn't long till I couldn't figure out who was who and what they were looking at. The only one I could keep track of was the tall guy who seemed to be in charge. He kept his eyes on me the whole time. After what seemed a very long time, but probably wasn't, I heard a voice in my head say "follow me." They all turned and walked towards the door, not even looking back to see if I was coming. Something told me to just go along and see what could possibly top what had already happened.

We didn't go far before entering another room much like the storage space I arrived in earlier. The biggest difference was that this one had some very old fashioned looking and very comfortable chairs arranged in a semi-circle with one seat in the center. The group took the row of seats, leaving me the choice of standing up or sitting in the center. Being an old Army guy, I chose to sit. A little explanation of that comment is in order. I was taught that a soldier never runs when he can walk, never walks when he can stand, never stands when he can sit, and never stays awake when he can sleep. That made sense to me then and it still does. I sat down and looked at the aliens facing me, wondering what was coming next. All the alien abduction stories I had heard or read about described being strapped down on a table with bright lights shining in your face. Scary aliens prodding you and probing your nether regions with a variety of instruments. Painful, scary, humiliating procedures that scarred your sensibilities and made you want to forget it even happened. To my surprise, the first thing that happened after we sat down was, they offered me refreshments!

An alien came in with a tray of milk and cookies. He started with the leader and offered each of us our choice from the tray. Again, my Army training kicked in and I took all the cookies left on the tray. When abducted by aliens, your next meal isn't guaranteed so you better get all you can while it's there to get. I thought: "How often do aliens eat?" "How often do they think we need to eat?" These random questions flashed through my mind as I sat there munching a cookie and wondering what would come next. Nothing was said until we all finished our snack. I put a couple of the cookies in my shirt pocket for later. This seemed to interest them a little. They put their heads together and I felt as much as heard a high pitched sound coming from them. I was to learn later that this is how they communicate among themselves. We would call it telepathy but it was much more than that.

The taller alien, the one I already thought of as the leader, started talking to me. He had a very pleasant voice with an Asian quality to it kind of like Mr. Sulu on Star Trek. "I guess you are wondering why we brought you here."

Since I was nodding in the affirmative, he went on. "We have been monitoring the earth experiment for a long time

5

now. Many thousands of your earth years have passed since we first seeded this planet with intelligent life. When we first came here there were several competing life forms that could have become the rulers of earth. We chose you. Like any experiment, we have experienced both success and failure. We even had to start over several times. You humans appear to have arrived at a point in your development that makes it necessary to decide if it's time to start over again. You were brought here so that we might hold a discussion of the facts of your case and arrive at an informed decision. You were chosen because our analysis of your DNA shows you to be the human that is closest to what we wanted our experiment to produce."

You can't imagine my surprise at this turn of events. What did they mean by start over? Were they considering wiping out the people of earth and then doing it all again? What could I possibly say or do to make them change their minds? The phrase: "anything you say can be held against you in a court of law flashed into my head." Since I have two ears and only one mouth, I decided to listen to the aliens and see what led up to this potential disaster. It was a sure thing that I'd better do some listening before I started talking. The fate of the human race might depend on it!

CHAPTER THREE

The Birth of Religion

While it may sound like science fiction, I swear that everything I have written here is my best recollection of what they told me. A lot of it sounds so weird that I couldn't make it up. I just don't have the imagination for that. The leader of the aliens began to tell me about where we came from.

In the beginning there was a herd of anthropoids that resembled humans but were more ape-like than modern people. They had no tools at all and just drifted around in a group eating about anything they could find. Since they had no tools or weapons, they couldn't kill anything, except by accident. They mostly ate nuts and berries, bugs and insects, and occasional left over's from some larger animal's kill. They existed this way for many thousands of years until the aliens came along and made a minor adjustment to their brains. It was a simple matter to manipulate the DNA of these primitives to stimulate new thought processes. This new way of thinking allowed them to make discoveries and generalize them to other situations.

Much like the anthropoids in 2001: A Space Odyssey, they started with a simple club. One of the anthropoids happened to have a short, heavy stick in his hand when members of another group tried to drive them away from a water hole. Up to this point in history, conflict consisted of wildly swinging your arms at the enemy while shrieking at the top of your lungs. Sooner or later someone would get scared and run away. This time when it happened, the stick happened to be in the anthropoids hands when he started wildly swinging his arms. The stick hit a member of the other group in the head, driving him to his knees and eventually resulting in his death. All the anthropoids were stunned. Because of the adjustments that the aliens made, the anthropoid with the club suddenly realized the value of the stick in his hand as a weapon. After killing the first enemy, he immediately gave chase and the other group ran away. The other members of his alien altered group also saw the value of the stick as a weapon and began to arm themselves as well.

With a club in hand, the pre-humans could also kill small animals and drive away some of the smaller predators that had been able to kill and eat them at will. That allowed this group of primates to consume more protein which in turn made them grow bigger and stronger as individuals and as a group.

Another discovery happened, seemingly by accident. One of the early humans cut his hand on the sharp edge of a freshly broken stone. Even as his hand bled, he picked up the stone and examined it closely. To see if this was a once in a lifetime occurrence or something useful, he banged the sharp rock against one of his fellow cavemen. Each time he hit him, more blood ran out. He kept hitting until the other caveman died of blood loss. His discovery had made him the most powerful member of his group. His joy and exalted position were to be short lived. Because of the adjustments to the brains made by the aliens, other members of the group caught on pretty fast. They began to search for sharp stones and discovered that certain types of rock were sharper than other types. They also discovered that they could actually chip off pieces of stone and create their own, even sharper weapons. The arms race was on. Little did anyone know that such a simple beginning would lead to eventual development of weapons of mass destruction, including the atom bomb! Wait. I am getting ahead of myself.

Most of these groups of humanoids rolled along using only the most basic tools for thousands of years. The aliens singled out a few of the more promising individuals and adjusted their brains, making them even more inquisitive and gave them a primitive language. This started the climb towards modern humans. By seeming accident, they discovered fire. At first, they found it occurring naturally as a result of lightning strikes or even volcanic action. Fire was a treasure to be guarded jealously. It is a point of argument as to whether the mastery of fire or the discovery of weapons (tools) was the most important step towards us becoming fully human. You can debate it for a month and not get a definitive answer. Since it is not really important to the story, let's move on.

In this primitive group, the person who maintained the fire became a sort of spiritual leader. That's where Og came in. Og was the first religious figure in the history of what would become man. He was the keeper of the fire in his group but wanted more. While the others were out hunting and gathering, Og stayed in camp tending the fire. If the fire went out, they would be cold and the meat they collected would be eaten uncooked. While they were very good at keeping a fire going, they really had no idea how to start one on their own. The aliens stepped in and gave Og the secret of fire. He could strike a spark from stones made of flint and create fire. This gave Og power over the other members of his group.

He talked of his contact with mysterious forces that no one else could see or hear. He was special and should be treated special. Soon, Og was given the choicest cuts of meat, and first pick of any nuts and berries brought into camp. Once he realized his powerful position, he decided that he should also have his pick of the women in the camp. This fit into the aliens plans perfectly. This allowed him to pass on the changes in his DNA that the aliens had given him. Although the primitives did not really understand what caused a child to be created, Og's exalted position within the tribe insured that his DNA would soon dominate the tribe's descendants.

Og made sure he maintained his position by creating rituals to impress the tribe. The rituals were said to make it possible for Og to speak to the gods and interpret their wishes for the tribe. He picked the cave bear, as "god" since every member of the tribe viewed that animal as one of the most powerful creatures in existence and that made the religious concept real to them.

The aliens thought they were on to something good. They decided to influence the development of some more early humans so they could speed up the spread of the altered DNA to subsequent generations. The aliens selected several suitable subjects from surrounding tribes and adjusted their brains. While they weren't sure how this would work out, they were willing to take a shot. After all, if it didn't work out, they could always start over. Time was on their side.

As the years passed, another smart caveman from a nearby group decided that if Og could do it, so could he. He saw that Og was onto something big. Og got all the best of everything, including the women. He decided he wanted some of that action. Zog the caveman figured that he could do everything

10

that Og did but he first needed to make a few changes. He would say his "god" was the saber toothed tiger. Zog would be the only one who could communicate with "god" so he should be viewed as special by the whole tribe. He would argue that his "god" was the strongest and only true god and so his tribe should believe and do only what he says. They should only believe the messages sent by the saber toothed tiger god and they should kill anyone who said different. This action unwittingly created the second religion and war at the same time.

The aliens pointed out to me that they had engineered a certain amount of aggression into human DNA. They pointed out that the greatest scientific and engineering advancements seem to come during periods of stress. Look at the leaps and bounds in technology caused by the two world wars. Humans went from flying in underpowered biplanes to jets, rockets, and even the atom bomb in just a few years. Amazing!

As time passed, more sharp operators saw the way to a great lifestyle was to create their own Religion. They would make subtle changes to prior religions and say that "god" spoke to them directly and told them that everyone else was wrong and this was the only true way to eternal reward. Thousands of years sped by and generations lived and died. Religion and war roaring along, hand in hand. I could grasp this concept as working to spread desired DNA during caveman times but what about today? When you look at how people have killed each other and are still killing each other in the name of religion I had to wonder if it really worked out as planned. I asked the aliens to tell me more of what they had seen as they monitored the human race over the years.

CHAPTER FOUR

Religious Evolution

The alien leader was quick to respond. Apparently they live very long lives because he described what went on as if he was actually there seeing it all happen. Since I was from a "Christian" country, he told me how Christianity developed over the centuries. The alien leader explained that each succeeding religion was based in part on the tenets of prior religions. For example: The Zorastrian religion emphasizes the eternal conflict of good versus evil. The Buddhists have celibate monks that shave their heads, renounce earthly wealth, lived in monasteries, and chanted with beads. The Hindu cult of Krishna emphasized the personal nature of god as a figure to be loved and worshiped. In ancient Greece, Bacchae sacrificed humans and ate the flesh and drank the blood. This is symbolized in Christianity by eating the bread and drinking the wine. Some forms of Christianity even say that once the bread and wine are sanctified, it turns into the actual flesh and blood of Jesus. The Egyptians worshiped Osiris who was murdered, resurrected, and then personally judged the dead. Jesus, who put the Christ in Christianity, was a Jewish Rabbi. Most of the Old Testament of the Christian bible is based on Hebrew/Jewish texts. I could go on but you get the picture.

Turning to the leader of the aliens I said: "You already told me that you started religion to help spread the altered DNA. Where did the plan go wrong?"

His detailed response really makes a lot of sense once you hear it described so simply. It seems that throughout history there were wildly divergent religions everywhere. Some worshiped the king or tribal leader. Some worshiped the sun, the moon, the stars, or all the above. Some had a veritable pantheon of gods that they worshiped for specific perceived needs. Many of them were very similar like Odin and Jupiter or the God of Thunder "Thor" and the Slavic Storm God "Perun". Most of the gods were specialized and seemed to have a staff of people on hand to receive appropriate offerings from the populace. If you had a specific problem, then you had to make offerings to pay off that specific god. No offerings meant there was no possibility of receiving help from that god. The plethora of gods was very confusing and very expensive. Something had to be done.

The aliens decided to introduce some new ideas into religion and see where that would take them. Up to that point in human history, most people worked every day. The only time they did not work was when the king declared a celebration and gave them time off. Obviously, these celebrations were very popular with most of the common people. The aliens noticed this phenomenon and decided to introduce two desirable changes to religion and then stood back to see what happened. What were these changes? They were very simple. They introduced the concept that there is only one God and then they added the weekly day off. You might wonder what the day off has in common with the worship of one God. The Jews seem to be the first major

13

group to recognize the one God concept. In their story of creation, God worked for 6 days and on the seventh day he rested. If it was good enough for God to rest one day in seven, then who are we to question it? They made the day off an integral part of their religion. In fact, it was a sin to work on the seventh day or Sabbath as it was named!

Imagine the joy of the common people. It was much cheaper to sacrifice to one God than to many. Add to this a religious requirement to take one day off out of every seven work days? That's a no brainer. Where do I sign up? Obviously, the kings and rulers of the day were somewhat put off by all this. The idea that the whole workforce should take off every seventh day was unheard of. How could they continue to amass vast amounts of wealth with everybody loafing one day each week? The poor working class jumped at the chance to embrace a religion with one God, time off every week, and an everlasting future in a heavenly environment after departing the earthly plane. Of course, the rulers on earth were against it from the start.

By this time I was getting a little tired. It was late when I arrived on the alien craft and who knows how long I had been there. The lights made it seem like daytime all the time. My eyes kept creeping shut and I was having a difficult time listening to the alien leader's soothing tone. At some point I must have dozed off.

While I was asleep, the big soft chair I was in turned into a bedlike recliner. I woke up feeling better than I had felt in a long time. None of the aliens were present but there was a plate of cookies and another glass of milk sitting on a small table by my chair. After I ate I noticed a curious looking cubicle built into the wall. It looked a little like a shower stall

14

only there were no handles to turn on the water. Just for the heck of it I stepped inside to take a closer look. Once inside, I saw that I was standing on the outline of two feet. Almost immediately, a soothing mist filled the cubicle. It wasn't like anything I ever felt before. It wasn't exactly wet but it didn't feel dry either. All I know is it felt pretty good, so I just stood there until the mist went away. To my amazement, I was clean all over. My hair was clean. My teeth were clean. Even my clothes were clean. Another intriguing thought occurred to me. I did not need to go to the bathroom. Anyone over the age of forty knows that we have to go to the bathroom quite often. What was going on here? I know that I was on the alien craft for hours, including a sleep period long enough to make me feel fully rested. My watch was no help since it stopped at the same time my motorcycle went dead back on earth.

While I stood there wondering, the alien leader entered the room. He was ready to go on with his report on the history of religion on earth but I had questions I wanted answered.

I blurted out: "How long have I been here? Why don't I have to use the bathroom?"

The alien leader responded: "You have been here for approximately twenty four hours as you measure time. While you were asleep, we adjusted your metabolism and repaired much of the damage living on earth has caused your body. The food and drink we provided you were totally absorbed by your body, leaving no waste matter."

I don't know about you but I have always felt younger than I am. I see other people my age and think how old they look but since I'm on the inside looking out, I never think of myself as old. After the alien leader told me they were repairing my body, I paused for a closer look. Everyone knows there are a number of little aches and pains that accumulate over the years and just become part of life. You really don't even notice them most of the time. Yet when I thought about it, those little aches and pains were gone! I broke my wrist when I was twenty and years later, sometimes it would ache so badly that it would wake me from a sound sleep. I tore the ACL in my left knee and it suffered small aches most of the time. My right shoulder was a mess from my years as a professional wrestler. Even my big toe demonstrated occasional shooting pains when I put pressure on it. Imagine my excitement when I realized that all the minor pains were gone! My pants were loose in the waist and my arms were bulging with muscle! Even the skin on my hands looked younger. I looked around for a mirror but there was none and I was too embarrassed to ask the alien leader for one so I could see if I looked as good – and young – as I felt. I was definitely looking forward to seeing myself in the mirror but decided I better put my curiosity on the shelf and let the alien leader get on with the story.

He began by talking about Rome. Take a look at the early Roman Empire and its epic battles to crush the one God believing Jews. For centuries the Romans ruled Judea, constantly fighting one Jewish based religious cult or another. If you want to see how committed they were to this goal, look at the Roman's assault on the Jewish stronghold at Masada. The Jews had a fortress on top of a rocky plateau on the western edge of the Judean Desert, overlooking the Dead Sea. It had excellent aqueducts carved into the living stone to collect the seasonal rains for consumption later. They had enough weapons stored there for about ten thousand warriors. There was plenty of food as well. Three precarious trails wove their way to the top and were blocked by heavy gates. This was a tough nut to crack. Undaunted, the Romans laid siege to this fortress, trapping several hundred members of a splinter group of extremist Jews on the plateau. The Romans built a wall all the way around the plateau then constructed an earthen ramp so they could launch an assault on the fortress. It is estimated that nine hundred and sixty Jews committed suicide rather than be enslaved by the conquering Romans. Their defiant stand has been a symbol and beacon to Jews ever since.

When the Jewish religion morphed into Christianity, the Romans did all they could to stamp them out, even feeding them to wild animals in the arena. Of course they also had other, more imaginative ways to kill them. Sometimes they would pit a group of Christians against a group of Amazons or dwarfs or a group of criminals. Sometimes they made them fight each other. You say this is despicable, but consider that the Christians did exactly the same thing to the unbelievers (non-Christians) just as soon as they were in power! That should give you something to think about.

Later, another group became the champion of belief in one God. They are the Muslims. Although the Jews, Christians, and Muslims all cling to belief in only one true God, and share common ancestry, they have been mortal enemies almost all their existence. Read the Old Testament, the Torah, and the Koran and you see that the stories are very similar. It's the details that cause all the problems. The Jews don't think the Messiah has come yet. The Christians say that unless you believe in Jesus you will suffer in Hell throughout eternity. The Muslims mention Jesus as a prophet but have their own road to heaven. Early on, the Muslims recognized Christians and Jews as believers in One God. Because of this, they were tolerated in Muslim territories. True, they were treated as second class citizens and had to pay a special tax but they were not killed outright for their difference in beliefs.

For obvious reasons, the Christians, in the form of the early Catholic Church, seemed to forge close ties with their contemporary kings and monarchs. They had an enormous amount of influence over earthly rulers while trying to maintain the appearance of separation. The Catholic Church appears to be expert at manipulating the rules to favor their dreams of universal control. There has always been a lot of controversy concerning which writings would be accepted as "books" in the official Christian Bible. Some of the books that were considered by the Catholic Church, but not included in the Bible, make up the "Apocrypha". Other religious writings were considered so troubling that they were burned and anyone caught with them or spreading their "heresy" was killed. Since it was the early Catholic Church that selected the text that would become the universally accepted Bible, they could have put anything they wanted in it – and did.

Personally, I have always wondered about the focus on earthly obedience to the laws of man and the responsibility for tithing and offerings to the Church clearly outlined and stressed by the teachings of the Church. Could they have been playing up to the earthly rulers by telling the people to be meek and humble and to obey their God anointed rulers in return for a happy afterlife? "Give to Caesar what is Caesar's." "The meek shall inherit the earth." If I wanted to keep the people in their place, I would have been sure to add some advice like this to my religious doctrine.

Me and the alien leader seemed to be getting along pretty well. It dawned on me that he never gave me his name and I never asked for it. I simply thought of him as the alien leader.

I decided that I better ask him before things went much further. "What's your name?"

He replied: "Names are an outmoded concept within our society. We normally communicate on a level which you would describe as telepathy so names are not needed. To make it simple for you, just call me Elroy."

"OK Elroy! Now that's out of the way, please proceed with your lecture."

For centuries, if you needed to know something about the Bible, the priest would tell you. They discouraged reading and the pursuit of knowledge by people outside the Church. No need to waste your time reading and thinking for yourself. That just led to problems. The priest will tell you what you need to know so don't ask questions.

It has been written that the early Catholic Church allowed its priests to marry. The Church hierarchy noticed that priests seemed to accumulate a lot of material wealth which they left to their families. God is said to have told the Pope that it would be better if priests did not marry and all their material possessions should be inherited by the Church. That change greatly increased the wealth and power of the Catholic Church. Whether these details are true or not is lost in history. The fact remains that priests could marry, and then they couldn't.

The Catholics have always taken the long view. Instead of trying to stamp out older holidays that had been around for years, they simply put their holidays on the same date as the old celebrations. After a period of time, the original reason for the celebration would have been forgotten. It was as if the earlier celebration never existed.

By ruling that no one is allowed to practice any form of birth control, they hoped to breed their way to a dominant position in the world. The Bible does say, 'Be fruitful and multiply.' Did they include this as part of their plan to breed their way to dominance? The Catholic Church has been in existence for close to two thousand years now, with no end in sight. In strong Catholic areas of the world, the population is exploding. However, with the growth of science and the spread of literacy, the power of the Catholic Church has been severely diminished from its peak a few centuries ago but it is still plugging away hoping to get back on top.

CHAPTER FIVE

Christians go to War

Up to this point, I had read about many of the things the alien leader told me. I just never put it all together so I could see the pattern that developed over centuries. Elroy continued.

During the middle ages, the Catholic Church again made a major move. In 1095, Pope Urban the Second preached for the first holy crusade. They decided that since the infidel Muslims controlled Jerusalem, the most holy city in the Christian religion, that a Crusade was in order. Thousands of people immediately "took the cross" and set out for the Mideast.

The rules of the Crusade were very similar to the much maligned Jihad of the Muslim faith. If you died while participating in the Crusade, all your sins were forgiven, and you automatically went to heaven! This is eerily similar to the Muslim promise of Heaven for giving your life during Jihad. The Church also promised to control all your property, just like it was their own, while you were gone on the Crusade. It took about a year or more to travel to that part of the world from Europe. You would spend a year or so killing infidels, and then make your way back home. You would be gone at least three years, if you came back at all. Of course, if you died during the Crusade, your property would be abandoned, and become the property of the Catholic Church. The Christians who took part in the Crusades used this time to not only kill Muslims, but to kill any Jews or other undesirables that crossed their path. After all, they were doing God's work. This went on for about two hundred years and through four major and five minor crusades. The last Christian city in the Holy Land, Acre, fell in 1291. The dream of returning to the Holy Land nonetheless proved popular. The Kings of France and England frequently made plans for more crusades, though in nearly every case the crusades were derailed by regional tensions.

The Crusades were an important factor in the history of the progress of civilization. The effects of the Crusades increased the wealth and power of the Catholic Church; increased their influence on political matters, commerce, intellectual development, society at large, and also prompted the famous voyages of discovery. The crusades exposed Europeans to a number of exotic ideas and products they had never seen before. The "Saracens" as they were called by the crusaders, bathed regularly, used a variety of spices the Europeans had never tasted, and had advanced medical techniques that were viewed with suspicion by the invaders. Their math, science skills, and knowledge of astronomy were very advanced for the time period.

One major side effect of the crusades was the opening of trade and the introduction of new products to European markets. The lessons learned from this made the Catholic Church support voyages of discovery that eventually opened up the New World of the Americas. Their excuse was the spreading of god's word while their eyes were on the gold, silver, and jewels to be found in the hands of the natives.

To really secure their grasp of religious and secular power, the Catholic Church created the Inquisition. In 1184, at

Languedoc, in the south of France, the first Inquisition was initiated to ferret out heretics or offenders of Canon Law. Early in the thirteenth century, Pope Gregory IX assigned the duty of performing the Inquisition to the Dominican Order. They were allowed to use torture to draw out confessions from suspected heretics. By their rules, they could not draw blood while making you confess. This limited them to use of the rack, breaking of various bones, and the clever use of red hot metal utensils among other ingenious torture methods. Depending on the Inquisitor in charge, it was not uncommon to execute someone immediately after confession and forgiveness. They viewed that as merciful since it kept the person from sinning again and thereby losing their place in heaven.

I commented, "You have to admire their thoughtfulness."

Even as I said this I was unsure if Elroy understood sarcasm. Since his expression never seems to change, it's hard to tell. He continued with his historical observations.

By the start of the sixteenth century the Catholic Church had reached a dominant position as the established religious authority in western and central Europe. They dominated the other players which included Judaism, and the Spanish Muslims. These groups hardly figured in terms of numbers or political and religious influence. That's when the real trouble started. In 1517, Martin Luther published his work, *The Ninety-Five Theses* and started the Protestant Reformation. This started a number of religious turf wars that would last until the Treaty of Westphalia in 1648. You could also throw in the story about how King Henry of England declared himself the God anointed head of the Anglican Church. After all, the Catholic Pope refused to give him a divorce from his Catholic wife.

What's a King to do? This made England a Protestant nation forever more. At least King Henry had a logical reason for his actions.

From Elroy's stories, I knew the aliens could see this wasn't working out like they planned. They thought that the whole "one God" idea would simplify things and bring people together. They had high hopes for the followers of the Rabbi Jesus whose teachings morphed into Christianity. They forgot the lessons of Og and Zog.

Elroy pointed out: "Any time someone has a good thing going, someone else is going to want a piece of the action." Look at America today. Everywhere you look you see another church. Most of them are loosely based on the original Christian theme. A look at their names will give you a peek at the mind set of those who worship there. Names like 'The True Word of Jesus Apostolic Church', Church on the Rock (of Jesus)', 'King James Bible Evangelic Tabernacle' and more. Heck, I expect to see 'The Real Word of Jesus Christ – All Others Will Burn in Hell – Church of the Revealed Gospel' as the name of a storefront church. The probable reason you don't see that everywhere is there are too many words to fit on their sign.

Everyone who has ever used an office copier will understand this example. If you copy the original, then the copy looks almost the same as the original. If you copy a copy, then the image is worse than the original. Every generation away from the original looks progressively more different than the original. Apply this to your view of the various 'Christian' churches springing up. While they all purport to be Christian, compared to the original, they are barely recognizable. Look at the Church of Jesus Christ of Latter Day Saints or the Mormons as you commonly call them. If you read what they actually believe, then most people would consider them to be not only nuts, but a cult.

Elroy began to describe their beliefs. "The following is the most important teaching of Mormonism. It is one of the Fourteen Articles of Faith that they follow. They believe that God was once a mortal man on another planet who progressed by living in obedience to the laws and ordinances of the gospel he had on his world. After he died, he was resurrected and evolved to become a god. He then created this world. They believe that you can follow in God's footsteps by becoming perfect and then you will become Gods and Goddesses ruling other worlds. "

Until Donny and Marie and the rest of the Osmond's became regulars on network television, they had little positive national exposure. The squeaky clean image the Osmond's displayed probably did more to make people accept the Mormons as a real religion than anything up to that time. If Donny and Marie could be Mormons, then it was probably a real religion after all.

The message each new church seems to preach is that because of a private chat they had with God, they were directed to let you know that they and they alone are right, and all others will be denied a place in heaven since everyone else is being mislead by the Devil!

All this information was making my head spin. I had never really taken a close look at religion or the different denominations and how they interacted with governments and with each other. Suddenly my mind was open to ideas that I never considered before.

I have always wondered why all churches place so much stress on tithes and offerings? If God created the heavens and the earth from nothing, does he really need ten percent of what we earn? They say that tithes are what we owe God. You pay what you owe first. Then if you give more, it becomes an offering. The televangelists are experts at getting people to send them money. One of my favorite religious hucksters would sit in a rocking chair, smoking a pipe and read to the audience about ghosts or flying saucers. When he would get to an exciting part, he would stop reading and tell the TV audience that he wouldn't proceed until the phones started ringing and he had pledges of another $10,000. He would then have his choir sing the same song over and over until the money was pledged.

Another shyster would send elderly Christians who lived on a fixed income a loan application with instructions on how to fill it out. I personally read one such appeal. The televangelist wanted the little old lady on Social Security to borrow $100 and send it in immediately. She could then make a payroll deduction from her meager Social Security check to pay back the loan in twelve easy payments. Praise the Lord! An all powerful God of Love should be able to make it without our help. It all sounds a lot like "Og-ism" to me. That's all I'm saying.

CHAPTER SIX

America – No Second Chance

After hearing Elroy deliver all these historical observations my mind started cataloging and pumping out information. I found myself asking questions and making statements about things that I wasn't really aware that I even knew about. Elroy told me that this was a partial result of the repairs they made. Our human brains are capable of lots of things that we never use them for. A slight brain adjustment by the aliens made me see things in a whole new way. I took over the lecture from Elroy and began to speak.

If one of the basic platforms preached by Jesus was forgiveness of others, when did this concept get lost? America has more laws, more offenses that are felonies and more people locked up than any so called civilized nation on the planet. By 2009, the prison population of America was 743 per 100,000 citizens. The second largest prison population belongs to Russia with 577 per 100,000. Our neighbor Canada only incarcerates 117 per 100,000. Even our current nemesis, Red China only locks up 120 per 100,000 of their citizens yet we constantly condemn them for human rights violations. America has just five percent of the world's population yet almost a quarter of all the world's inmates are locked up in America.

Some of the reasons for this are mandatory sentencing, longer sentences for similar crimes, and the proliferation of crimes that are considered a felony. Every time a crime gets significant media attention, you can bet the spin-off will be new legislation making something a felony. The recent Casey Anthony trial, and her subsequent not guilty verdict on the most serious charges, outraged the media and incited the populace to the point that at least two new felonies were added to the books.

There are always politicians that are ready to jump on the band wagon and show they are 'tough on crime.' In case the exact situation ever presents itself again, not likely but just saying, the defendant could have been charged with the new felonies of failure to report a child's death immediately and failure to report a child missing within forty eight hours. In the state of Tennessee, dueling legislators filed competing bills. When one legislator heard that a bill had been passed to require you to report a missing child within forty eight hours, the other legislator immediately filed a tougher bill requiring a report within twenty four hours. Neither considered the impact on local law enforcement office's that could be flooded with reports by people who don't want to be charged with a felony. Most law enforcement agencies won't even accept a missing person's report until twenty four to forty eight hours have passed. Their experience has shown that most people turn up within that time period.

History also shows that most missing persons are not actually missing. Most missing persons are actually a result of miscommunication when one party doesn't do a good job of keeping the other party informed. These new laws will create a lot of problems and will do very little to make America safer.

Many of the uninformed want these new laws in place, so that even if prosecutors couldn't prove guilt for the actual murder, they could still stack up significant time in jail for the two new felonies.

Their thinking is that if you are charged and arrested, then you must be guilty. Only the work of a really shifty lawyer can get you off. In this case, the "shifty lawyer" and lack of physical evidence got the defendant out of the most serious charges. The prosecutor types still want the tools to punish that defendant even when found innocent. Obviously, if the defendant wasn't guilty, then they wouldn't have arrested her. Right?

Our history is full of innocent people who were found guilty for little to no reason. Politicians want crimes solved, with cases closed quickly. How many people are forced to plead guilty to a lesser charge for fear they will be found guilty of a more serious crime that they know they did not commit? Another reason could be they can't afford a decent lawyer and are advised by their court appointed or otherwise low budget lawyer not to take a chance.

Prosecutors want a conviction. They charge a person with the toughest felony in that product line so they can negotiate it down to secure a conviction. That way they can preserve their high conviction rate. To the outsider it looks like the prosecutor is a veritable fountain of legal expertise while he is actually a manipulator of the criminal system who probably has aspirations to higher office. This happens a lot more than you think.

In our current, 'everything should be a felony' atmosphere, you could be a felon if you spank your child and someone reports you. Invasive pat downs by TSA agents trying to do

29

their duty at the nation's airports, could be a felony. When dealing with illegal aliens (mostly Mexicans, not the outer space kind) renting a house, assisting them to find work, or driving them around in your car, could be a felony. It all depends on what state you are doing it in. Most agree that it is terrible parenting to leave a child alone in a car while they run inside a store for a few minutes to shop. Does it rise to the level of a felony? If something happens to your child while alone in a car like that, then you will probably be charged with a felony.

A woman in Georgia was jaywalking so she could get home quicker from a hard day at work. She had just gotten off a bus while accompanied by her three children. The children darted into the street ahead of their mother. One was hit by a car and killed. The driver sped away. The mother was charged and convicted of vehicular homicide because she didn't escort the children three tenths of a mile to the nearest cross walk before crossing the street. She could have received a three year sentence for this crime. The hit and run driver, who had two previous hit and run convictions, admitted drinking earlier in the day while taking pain medication received a six months sentence. Did anyone really intend that a jaywalker be charged with vehicular homicide in a case like this when the law was written? I hardly think so. However, as the prosecutor stated: "these cases are inherently difficult because they are unintentional, but the state is bound to uphold the law." Because she clearly broke the law by jaywalking, she placed herself in jeopardy of being a felon. So next time you contemplate jaywalking or some other minor infraction, remember that in today's America, "minor" is in the eyes of the beholder (or prosecutor).

A few years ago a friend of mine let me in on a federally funded program called 'Make a Felony' or something similar to that title. This was a program that taught local police how to invent a reason to pull you over then develop probable cause to charge you with a felony. It was highly successful and resulted in quite a number of new felony arrests. How many normal families have placed a pistol under the seat or in the glove compartment for family protection while traveling? Thousands if not millions of normal people have done this. I'm talking about Sunday school teachers, Scout Leaders and others who are pillars of the community. You have no intentions of doing anything wrong. You just want to be prepared in case of trouble and want to be able to protect your family. You may even think you have a constitutional right to do so. Take that pistol across state lines and you may have committed a felony. Of course it depends on the laws of the state you are in, but are you a lawyer and expert on the laws of every state in America?

There are so many examples of things that may be felonies if they want them to be. During the "Make a felony" programs, they look for any excuse to make a case.

Sometime in 1990, I was driving a pickup truck in south Texas, about one hundred miles from the border. The local sheriff, with assistance from various law enforcement agencies, decided to stop all the cars traveling that highway on that day. They stood in the middle of the road and flagged everyone down (including me), motioning for everyone to pull over. The only thing the cars had in common was that they were traveling on that road, on that particular day. The police walked up and down the line of cars with a dog on a leash glaring at the occupants of the cars. "Stay in your cars with your hands where we can see them" they directed. As they walked up to

31

the window with one hand on their pistol, they shouted, roll down all your windows. They looked in all the windows while the dog sniffed around the outside of the cars. I asked them what they were looking for. "Illegal aliens," (again it was Mexicans and not the other kind) was their reply. "Do you mind if we look under your seat and in your glove compartment?" I really don't believe that anyone is dumb enough to think that a whole Mexican could be hiding under the seat of my Silverado pickup or in the glove compartment. Obviously, they were looking for something else. "Yes Officer, I do mind," I replied. Then a whole crowd of police officers gathered around my pickup, holding one hand on their pistols and glaring at me. "What's the matter boy? Don't you want law and order in America?" they asked. I replied: "I love America and proudly served in the Army during Vietnam, but I don't see how a Mexican can possibly have slipped into my glove compartment or under my seat without me knowing about it. Since you say you are looking for Mexicans, then I assure you that I have nothing to hide." They talked to each other for a few minutes, accompanied by a lot of arm waving and pointing, and then they finally told me to hit the road. "We'll be watching you!" were the last words I heard as I carefully pulled back onto the highway and drove away. I haven't driven in Texas since.

In places like California, per state law, you can legally buy medical marijuana at government taxed and licensed shops. The federal government can still charge you with a federal felony because they don't recognize the states right to make that call. What is a felony in one state may not even be a crime in another state.

Ask most "Christians" if a convicted felon should be able to have a decent job or live in their neighborhood, they will tell you NO! Good jobs and nice neighborhoods should be for people like them. If not by their words, then by their actions they follow the concept of "one strike and you are out." Their very prim and superior answer is that the convict should have thought of that before they broke the law.

Have you ever noticed that many times, the Christian with the worst case of religion is the person that was wildest in their pre-Christian years? From time to time I used to hang out at a local outlaw bikers club. I was never a member but I was a "friend of the club." That's because a couple of the guys worked for me at the local Army base and several more did business at my video store which was located about a mile from the clubhouse. Most of them were good guys but I admit that a few of them were a little wild. That is where I saw the following example of a woman who owned a local restaurant and then got the religion. After her conversion, she refused to sell beer or other alcoholic drinks in her restaurant because "Jesus" told her it was a sin. She was very sanctimonious in her actions with everyone she encountered. You would think she was now, and had always been, a regular Christian saint. My fondest memory of that lady was just a couple of years old. She used to be a regular visitor at the local outlaw biker clubhouse. That pretty much meant that she was available to tend to the sexual needs of the club members or anyone else they happened to bless with their permission. I remember her willingly "pulling the train" on the back room pool table one night. The only reference to Christianity was when she yelled "Oh God, Oh God" from time to time as she encouraged them in their efforts.

33

With a beatific look on their face, many of the most judgmental Christians are fond of saying "What would Jesus do?" Jesus would do as he did with Mary Magdalene when he said, "Let ye who is without sin cast the first stone" or when he forgave the thief on the cross next to him and said, "Tonight you will join me in the kingdom of heaven." That is what Jesus would do.

Jesus was once asked by the Rabbi's why he wanted to hang out with the common people? They said that if he was a good man, he should want to be with them because they were righteous men. His response was that they were already good and righteous men and didn't need him. He walked among the people because they needed him to be an example of righteousness that they could emulate.

You can tell that this is a paraphrase of what was said. Any good Christian will let you know in a minute that they all spoke Shakespearian English in biblical days. The proof is in the wording of the King James Version of the Bible. A lot of modern mouth breathers think that the King James Bible fell out of the sky as a gift directly from God. They think it is the only real, true word of God and all others are tainted by the hand of man. I know people who will fight you over the King James Version of the Bible and where it came from. I hate to admit it but some of them are actually related to me.

One day I was walking on a treadmill at the local gym. There were two guys on treadmills on either side of me carrying on a loud conversation about the joys of Jesus. Most of the information they were sharing was the most ignorant drivel I have ever heard. Their lack of knowledge about the history of Christianity was appalling. I listened to them expound until I just couldn't stand it anymore. Unfortunately, I tried to introduce them to the facts. I told them that Christianity was based primarily on ancient Hebrew texts and that the Catholics chose the books that made up the Christian Bible. They would not believe any such thing. God gave them the Bible and no one should add to it or take away from it. They were utterly convinced that I was the spawn of the Devil. Later on I found out that both of them were ministers. These two idiots were the leaders and teachers of their respective flocks. This is a prime example of the blind leading the blind. Their slogan should be, "say it out loud, I'm dumb and I'm proud!"

By this time I was beginning to get a little restless. After all, you can only talk for so long before you need a change of scenery. It may have been a result of the little adjustments the aliens did to me while I slept but I really wanted to learn new things. I was like the movie robot in "Short Circuit" who kept asking for input. I asked Elroy if he would show me around the ship. He said sure and off we went.

As we walked, a lot of things occurred to me that I probably wouldn't have even thought about before. There seemed to be gravity so I didn't float around. I could actually walk along normally. You could see everywhere you went but there was nothing like a light fixture anywhere in sight. The hallways had one curved wall so I guessed that they ran around the outside of the craft. Elroy lead me into the room that was at the end of the hallway. It was a control room of some sort. There were monitors with displays on them and all sorts of levers and buttons on consoles around the room. It kind of reminded me of the bridge of the Enterprise on the old Star Trek series. There were both windows and screens that provided you with visual information. There were a number of aliens in the room manning the various stations. It was difficult

35

to tell if these were the same ones I met earlier or a different group altogether. They all looked so similar.

As time passed, I noticed a strange thing happening. Even though they all looked similar, I began to detect slight differences in their appearance that helped me to tell them apart. I still didn't have names for any of them besides the leader Elroy but it was amazing to me that now I could actually tell them apart!

There was an almost electric hum in the air as they went about their jobs, in constant communication with the others in their group.

Elroy said: "This team fly's the ship and monitors all the flights originating from the earth's surface. When the earthlings first developed the ability to fly, we were very disturbed. It was hard enough to keep up with their comings and goings without the ability to fly to points all around the globe."

He pointed to three aliens working off to the side who were peering intently into a large flat screen. "They are monitoring the nuclear capabilities of the nations of earth. The proliferation of the means to launch nuclear weapons is one of the indicators that it could be time to start over. Several thousand years ago, humans developed nuclear capabilities and we thought it best to wipe them out and start again. You can still see traces at Mohenjo-Daro in India where modern archaeologists found skeletons that had radiation readings fifty times that normally expected and similar to the readings from Hiroshima and Nagasaki in modern times."

Many questions sprang to mind concerning what the ship was capable of. How fast could it travel? Was it a warship or was it just a scientific observation platform? Was there a deadline for making the decision on the future of the human race? These questions and many others popped into my head but I seemed to be driven to continue my observations about earthly religion. Elroy must have been telepathically nudging me to speak more about my own religious observations but at the time I really wasn't aware that they could influence our thoughts without us being aware of it. We walked back to the original room, had some lunch, and I continued my diatribe on the evolution of religious attitudes on earth.

CHAPTER SEVEN

Religious Separatism

I believe that Jesus' words to the Jewish church leaders have been forgotten in modern times. At least by their actions, modern Christians seem to want to distance themselves from regular folks. By regular folks, I refer to the common crowd that might go to church on special occasions but are by no means devout followers of modern Christianity. Part of it comes from fear that the morals of the great unwashed will rub off on them. Some of it is probably racially motivated.

When forced integration swept the nation, it was amazing how many church operated schools sprang up. They will of course protest that it wasn't racism, but a desire for a godly setting for their children's education that all these church schools provide. Many of them will actively seek a few minority students so they can proudly point them out as examples of their sophistication and dedication to political correctness.

The Christians didn't stop there. They got involved in marketing and discovered that in addition to Christian schools, there was a desire for Christian sports complexes, Christian day care centers, gyms, sports programs, counseling centers and more. From this market research sprang the modern Mega-Church. You see them in every town now. They offer everything that any local community offers. They have thousands of members who do not want to rub elbows with non-Christians as they worship and participate in recreation activities within their closed community. A lot of them have their own television shows which they produce in their own studios. That allows them to reach out and spread their brand of Christianity to even more people.

I suppose that there is a certain level of comfort from being a part of a herd like that. You don't have to think for yourself because there will always be someone around to tell you how to fit in. Some of these churches have gone so far as to publish a book of Christian Businesses that the membership is encouraged to support. God forbid that you should buy a widget from a non-Christian widget store. I guess they forgot that setting a good example while out among the heathen could help save the souls of the sinners. It must be better to avoid contamination by the sinners than it is to set a good example for them to emulate.

When I was young, these mega-churches were not common yet. The little country church we went to could only afford a preacher every other Sunday. We had preaching every first and third Sunday and usually went to another country church down the road for preaching every second and fourth Sunday. The preacher had another country church he worked when we couldn't afford him.

He was "called" to preach. He was not a college educated preacher with a Master of Divinity Degree. When the preacher and his family appeared in our community, a different family would take them home to feed them and give them a place to spend the night. That preacher had a day job as well so he could support his family. He definitely didn't enter the ministry for the money and glamour. His call to preach placed a burden of responsibility on him and on his family. He made a personal sacrifice and his family shared in the sacrifice required to allow service as a good shepherd. I'm not so sure about the motives of many of today's ministers.

High salaries, expense accounts, church owned cars, subsidized housing and more are perks that pastors expect and receive these days. I'm sure they still believe they are sacrificing something to serve as a minister but I just don't see what that is.

Elroy asked me to describe how the modern practice of Christianity impacted my life. He was trying to understand if the way Christianity was practiced today was better than in the past. After all, the one god concept was an idea that they planted over two thousand years ago. The aliens wanted to hear my personal observations so they could see what it had developed into.

CHAPTER EIGHT

What Happened to Christian Charity?

While there seems to be a lot of talk about Christian charity, the way they practice it today rubs me the wrong way. We were about the poorest family in the community when I was growing up. Many times we would find a sack of groceries or a bag of hand-me-down clothes that someone in the community had outgrown, on the back seat of our car when we came out of the old church. No one ever made it a point to tell us who gave us these things. Giving was a private thing. It was not something that you made a fuss about. That old church didn't have air conditioning or padded benches. You had to walk up the hill to an outhouse because they didn't even have running water. What it did have was a group of people who exhibited the truest example of the Christian spirit I have ever seen.

It still rubs me the wrong way when people give to charity and want a receipt for their taxes. If you only give something to get a tax cut, it is not really charity at all. The whole concept of charitable giving rubs me the wrong way these days. A lot of national charities exist only for the purpose of raising money.

After the devastating events of 9/11, the Red Cross raised over $40,000,000 in donations for assistance to the families of the nearly 3,000 people who died there. A year later, not a dollar of that money had been distributed to those who needed it. That information was revealed on a news exposé on television but the meaning didn't sink into the minds of the masses. Agencies like the Red Cross still use any excuse to raise money that does not reach the needy for which it was intended. In another television exposé, the Red Cross was again slammed for raising money during an epidemic of wild fires in California. They had film of a person's house burning in the background as they asked the public to contribute. The friends of the home owner called her to say how great it was that she was helping the Red Cross raise money even as her home burned. She was not aware of any of this and she was never offered any help from the Red Cross. Fortunately, she was a lawyer and took action on her own to stop this kind of fund raising. Since news programs are for those with limited attention span, they never came back and told us the results of the lawyer's efforts.

For most people, it is just a matter of convenience. They know these are national charities and it makes them feel like they have done something good to make a contribution. They don't really care what is done with the money and assume that it is doing someone some good. My advice is that you find an individual who needs help and help him or her. That way you know your money is going to assist someone in need and is not going to keep a high paid staff in opulent surroundings. Most people are astonished when they really take a look at the national charitable organizations and what they spend their money on. One of my relatives told me that during the Korean War, his troop ship landed and the first thing they saw was the Red Cross on the dock selling them coffee and doughnuts. Not giving them coffee and doughnuts. They were selling them. Back home in the States, they were having huge fund raising drives so they could support our boys over there.

This kind of charitable giving is similar to giving your money to most of today's religious groups. After they have financed their huge buildings, gyms, sports programs, high salaries and so on, if there is something left over, they might consider helping someone outside their church that is in need. That is highly unlikely however, because a new rule that has crept into their thinking is that they should only help their own members. I recently helped a single working mother purchase school supplies for her children. She had already asked for assistance from every big church in town. They all told her that they only helped members of their church. Imagine that. What would Jesus do?

Karl Marx actually said, "Religion is the sigh of the oppressed creature, the heart of a heartless world, and the soul of soulless conditions. It is the opium of the people." This is usually paraphrased, "Religion is the opiate of the masses."

The alien leader Elroy said: "Ever since Og the Caveman, religion has existed and there always seems to be a market for more. The unintended consequence is that more war and death has occurred during human history because of religious differences than for any other reason."

I began to see the impact of human religious practices on the decision the aliens were contemplating as they considered a "do over" for mankind.

I was mentally reeling from the memories of my own experiences and the alien's explanation of how religion was used by them to influence the actions of the people of earth. Religion started out as a good idea and had some early success, but somewhere along the way it all went awry.

43

CHAPTER NINE

The Rape of South America

Elroy asked me if I knew anything about how religion was used as the excuse for the conquest of the Americas. I really didn't know much about that part of history. I wasn't worried. How could you find a reason to want to wipe out human civilization and start over based on what happened years ago in South America? I was about to find out.

As Elroy described it, things weren't going too well in Europe so they (the aliens) made a few more mental adjustments to selected humans and the drive to explore was underway. Before this little adjustment, many of the people thought the world was flat. If you sailed too far, you would fall off the edge and probably be eaten by monsters. Of course they (the aliens) knew better so they planted the round earth idea in a few folks and stood back to see what happens next. They had high hopes that if you could start from scratch somewhere that things would be much better than in the recent past – what with the Crusades, the Inquisition, most of the royalty from European countries being cousins and all.. Again, it just didn't seem to work out. Not even at the start.

This team of aliens forgot about the work already being done in the Americas. It was probably because that was being supervised by another department. When the first Europeans arrived in the New World there were a lot of people already there. Since no accurate population records exist, there are estimates that are all over the charts. Some say there were between 30,000,000 and 54,000,000 people in South America; 2,000,000 to 18,000,000 in what would become the United States; and 200,000 to 2,000,000 in what became Canada. Any way you look at it, that's a lot of people in a "New World."

Sometime earlier, they (the aliens) adjusted the brains of the locals and these humans began to join together in larger and larger communities. These adjustments did not include the formula for making steel or for using the wheel but did allow them to accomplish some pretty amazing feats of construction. The first explorers to arrive were amazed to see great cities, roads, pyramids and such. They were also amazed when they learned of the religious rites practiced by the native inhabitants. Human sacrifice and wholesale slavery were common practice. The Catholic Church was having none of this!

An edict was issued by Pope Alexander VI in 1493 to the King and Queen of Spain following the voyage of Christopher Columbus to the island he called Hispaniola. This edict officially established Christian dominion over the New World. It called for the subjugation of the native inhabitants and their territories. It also divided all newly discovered or yet-to-be discovered lands into two parts. It gave Spain rights of conquest and dominion over one side of the globe and Portugal over the other.

The subsequent Treaty of Tordesillas (1494) re-divided the globe with the result that most Brazilians today speak Portuguese rather than Spanish, as in the rest of Latin America. These edicts have never been revoked, although the Vatican has been asked many times to consider doing so.

The newly arrived Europeans decided it was all theirs by divine right. When new diseases were introduced by the invaders, to which the local population had no natural immunity, the natives died by the millions. The European perception was that they operated under divine approval. They thought God removed the natives as part of His "divine plan" to make way for a new Christian civilization. Estimates run as high as a 90% mortality rate for the indigenous peoples of the Americas. This created one of the greatest human catastrophe's in history, far exceeding even the disaster of the Black Death of medieval Europe which killed up to one-third of the people in Europe and Asia between 1347 and 1351.

The natives did have some revenge as a particularly strong strain of Syphilis made its way home to Europe. It was primarily introduced by returning sailors from the voyages of Columbus who immediately spread it around the port cities. The first written records of an outbreak of syphilis occurred in 1494/1495 in Naples, Italy during a French invasion. Due to it being spread far and wide by returning French troops, it acquired the name "French disease." Until its strength had been diluted some by natural immunities being developed, this strain of syphilis usually killed within a few months.

If diseases weren't enough, the brutality of the Spanish Conquistadores is legendary. The Spanish treated their native subjects as something between slaves and serfs. Serfs stayed to work the land. Slaves were exported to the mines, where large numbers of them died. Some smaller tribes were simply wiped out, eliminating a hindrance to land use. At the same time, the attending priests did their best to convert the surviving natives to Catholic based Christianity.

From Elroy's description of the deplorable conditions most workers lived in, I can see why the Church always put so much emphasis on the great life Christians would have after they die. Life on earth just wasn't that good for a lot of the new converts. Their only hope was a better home in heaven.

One of the other aliens began to talk about what happened during the conquest of the Americas. War became deadlier after the arrival of the Europeans. Europeans had gunpowder and swords, which made killing easier and war more deadly. They were very successful in achieving domination in warfare with the natives for a variety of reasons. One reason was the staying power of the Europeans. The invaders had a highly developed supply network, and could sustain a conflict over several years. They could even fight in winter if necessary to accomplish their goals. Almost no native tribes had the stored resources to conduct a war for more than a few months.

Even though the massive death toll from disease played a major role in the European conquest, the invaders' approach to war was as important as it was new and different. The indigenous people waged war in a very ritualistic way. Individual prowess, demonstrations of bravery, even counting coup (touching an enemy without hurting him) were very important. The invaders were less ritualistic and more focused on achieving decisive victory. Death and destruction of the enemy was the goal of the European invader.

The Spanish conquerors charged around South America and Mexico killing the natives, making them slaves, and converting them to good little Catholics, all while looking for gold. The natives caught on pretty soon to the greed of the invaders. When asked where the gold, silver, and jewels were, the natives always said, 'There is a city of gold just over there.

The Conquistadors fell for it every time. Some of them actually walked from Mexico, through the Southwest portion of North America, and crossed Texas looking for the City of Gold. Francisco Coronado commanded an expedition which left from western Mexico in 1540. He was searching for the Seven Golden Cities of Cibola. Coronado did not find any golden cities, but discovered the Pueblo Indians.

By the time he had traveled all the way across Texas, Coronado was very upset at not finding the cities of gold. He split his men up and sent them off in different directions with orders to find the cities of gold. He knew they were there because the natives told him so. His men found the Grand Canyon instead. Coronado and his men then started moving east where he found only buffalo and grassy plains, but no cities of gold. Since he found no golden cities, Coronado claimed all the land over which he and his men traveled in the name of Spain.

I could see where the aliens were going. Yes, the early explorers and settlers were hard on the locals. Hasn't that always been the way though? Besides, most of what they are talking about happened in South America and Mexico didn't it. Were we that bad in the good old United States of America?

I was ready to find out what the aliens had to say about that but suddenly became aware of just how tired I was. Without another thought, I drifted off into a dreamless sleep.

I'm not sure how long I slept but when I woke up I was even more invigorated than before. Even though it doesn't seem possible, my body felt better than ever. Elroy and a group of three other aliens were in the room when I woke up so I asked them if they had been doing any more repair work to my body.

Elroy replied: "We have repaired all the damage to your body, reset your metabolism, and opened up large portions of your brain that had been unused. If you were on earth, you would find that you are about twice as strong as most earthlings and have the ability to telepathically influence the humans you encounter."

This revelation staggered me for a moment. Then Elroy added: "Since we have been observing you for a long time, we know of your interest in music. As a personal gift from our group we adjusted your brain to make you the consummate musician. You can now expertly play any earthly instrument and sing exactly as you desire."

If I was staggered before, this news practically made me lose my mind with joy! Obviously it was not possible to see any of this coming but this musical gift was like winning the lottery. Elroy and the group of aliens spread out and I could see a guitar sitting in a stand behind them. It appeared to be a Gibson Songwriter just like the one I had back home.

"Do you mind if I try it out?" Elroy replied: "We brought the guitar just so you could."

Without another word I hurried over to the guitar. It looked and felt exactly like the one I had back home. Even though I wondered if it was a real Gibson, I didn't ask. If the aliens could fly around in space and manipulate human DNA they could probably create a perfect copy of a Gibson guitar.

I have never been a great guitar player and always had to think about what I was doing. This made playing and singing at the same time very hard for me. Now my fingers seemed to have a mind of their own. Any song that I could think of seemed to jump from the strings. My fingers were flying up and down the neck creating chords that I had only dreamed of

49

before. When I started to sing it was also effortless. I could hit a range of notes and keys that had been impossible before the alien's musical gift to me. It made me wonder if Jimmy Hendrix or Jose Feliciano or Pete Frampton or Eric Clapton or any of the other legendary guitar players of my generation had also been "adjusted" by the aliens. While I wondered, I did not ask them. Some things are better if you don't know. I have always watched those guys as they made the music so effortlessly and wished that I could do it too. Thanks to the aliens, now I can.

I would have been happy to play and sing for hours but the alien group asked if we could get on with the human history discussion. It seems that they are getting pressure from their leaders to make a decision on our fate and no discussion would be complete without taking a long, hard look at the American experience.

CHAPTER TEN

Starting Over in America

America is the land of the free and the home of the brave! I felt pretty good about our chances now that the United States of America was the topic of discussion. Sure we have a few problems but we are still as good as it gets! Say "Amen" if you love America!

The aliens began by talking about the colony at Jamestown, Virginia which was established on May 14, 1607. This gave England its first foothold in the European competition for the New World. Before this, exploration and colonization were totally dominated by the Spanish.

Jamestown was started as a purely business endeavor. It wasn't until years later that things like religious freedom and individual rights made people want to come to America to live. Legend has it that the Indians welcomed the settlers with open arms. Most people believe that the local Indians gave food to the original settlers during the first winter and helped them to survive in the harsh new world. This spawned a celebration which became the annual holiday called Thanksgiving. Actually, there was very little formal contact with the Indians during that period of history. For the most part, the settlers stayed away from the Indians and the Indians stayed away from the settlers.

Theories abound about why the settlers found it so hard to survive in a veritable land of plenty. Some say the English settlers were so focused on finding gold and silver that they neglected to plant food and build adequate shelter for the first winter. Some say that the Algonquian tribe intermittently attacked the settlers keeping them focused on building a palisade for protection instead of planting food. We know that the Powhatan tribe did trade some food to the settlers for glass beads, copper, and iron implements.

The single minded focus on getting rich combined with the fact that many of the settlers were gentlemen who had never performed any common labor made it a miracle that any lived to tell the story. Mix all these circumstances together and you have a recipe for disaster. During the first few years, most of the settlers died. It was only through more and more replacements coming from Europe with more and more supplies, that they eventually reached a critical mass and were successful.

This all sounded reasonable to me. Over the years I have been interested in history and spent a lot of my spare time reading about it. When you take out the sentimental view of the relationship between the settlers and the Indians that most of us were taught in school, the alien's story sounded pretty accurate.

When the aliens started their description of slavery in the Americas, it was like nothing I had ever read or heard about.

CHAPTER ELEVEN

Slavery

A new member of the alien's group began the description of slavery. When most people think of slavery, they think only of the importation of black Africans. Most people don't realize that thousands of Indians were rounded up and sold off to work in the islands of the West Indies. Until the early 18th century, African slaves were difficult to acquire in the colonies that became the United States, as most were sold in the West Indies.

One of the first major establishments of African slavery in these colonies occurred with the founding of South Carolina in 1670. The colony was founded mainly by planters from the overpopulated sugar island colony of Barbados. They brought relatively large numbers of African slaves with them. For several decades it was still difficult to acquire African slaves in colonial America.

To meet labor needs, colonists had enslaved Indians for some time. They also developed the Indian slave trade during the late 17th and early 18th centuries by treating Indian slaves as a trade commodity to be exported. Most were sold to the West Indies. There are estimates that from 1670 to 1715, between 24,000 and 51,000 Indian slaves were exported from South Carolina alone. That was more than the number of

Africans imported to the colonies during the same period. Some say that Indian slaves were sold to the islands because they knew too much about their local surroundings. This enabled them to simply disappear into the wilderness. African slaves could not survive so easily in this strange new environment.

Slavery, introduction of new diseases, removal, and the European style of warfare pretty much devastated the indigenous people of North America. Most of the European settlers were men. The shortage of available women encouraged the European men to marry or otherwise fraternize with the native women. This is often overlooked as a reason for the diminished power of the local tribes. As this cross breeding increased, the original people were, to a large part, absorbed into the larger population.

Many of the southern colonies were penal colonies. They were settled by people forced to come to the New World. Most of those colonists were men. Most southern families of today can trace their family tree to one or more Indian ancestors. Usually, they are on the female side. It's an interesting phenomenon that most Southerner's are very proud of their Indian heritage while people from the Western states are looked down upon for having mixed blood. Maybe it's the perception that the eastern tribes were civilized Indians while the western tribes were "wild" Indians. That's a whole different subject.

For a number of reasons, Indians just didn't make good slaves in the new colonies. African slaves seemed to fill the bill for a required labor force. The first English colony in North America, Virginia, acquired its first African slaves in 1619, after a ship arrived, unsolicited, carrying a cargo of twenty to thirty

Africans. The practice of African slavery was established in the Spanish colonies as early as the 1560s. Most slaves were black and were held by whites, although some Indians and free blacks also held slaves. There were even a small number of white slaves as well. While the Europeans also held some Indians as slaves, they preferred to use them as trade goods.

Slavery spread to the areas where there was good-quality soil for large plantations of high-value cash crops, such as tobacco, cotton, sugar, and coffee. By the early decades of the 19th century, the majority of slaveholders and slaves were in the southern United States. Most slaves were engaged in a work-gang system of agriculture on large cotton and sugar cane plantations. Large groups of slaves were thought to work more efficiently if directed by white overseers.

Growing up during the civil rights movement in America, I heard a lot of diatribe concerning the evils of slavery. If it was so inherently evil, and Americans are so inherently good, then why did they do it? Since the aliens were there observing the whole thing, I asked them to explain it to me.

The alien briefing on slavery continued. The first, large numbers of African slaves came from Barbados. They already had experience working the sugar plantations so they could go right to work. European settlers in North America turned to African slaves as a cheaper, more plentiful labor source than indentured servants (who were mostly poor Europeans).

One of the major considerations that went into the decision to purchase African slaves was the comparatively high cost of European labor. A European laborer cost about seventy cents a day. In 1638, the average African slave only cost twenty seven dollars. In other words, you could recover the initial cost of your slave in forty days or less and then work them for almost nothing until they dropped dead.

Another factor was the improving economy in Europe which gave laborers less reason to brave the perils of the New World.

Though it is impossible to give accurate figures, some historians have estimated that six to seven million slaves were imported to the New World during the 18th century alone. They were mostly captured by other African tribes and sold or traded to Europeans that brought them to the New World for sale. Most of these ended up in the West Indies but it is estimated that from 450,000 to 600,000 eventually ended up in the American colonies.

At one point, when the land producing tobacco was wearing out, it looked like slavery would become commercially non-viable. Then Eli Whitney invented the cotton gin. That invention reinvigorated huge, southern farms and created the need for vast numbers of slaves to tend the fields. The cotton gin revolutionized the cotton industry by increasing fiftyfold the quantity of cotton that could be processed in a day.

Slaves in the North typically worked as house servants, artisans, laborers and craftsmen, with the greater number in cities. The agricultural South had a significantly higher number and proportion of slaves in the population, as its commodity crops were labor intensive.

An interesting aside is that many of the importers of slaves were ship owners from the North. They fostered a competition that lasted for years trying to build faster and faster ships so that slaves could be delivered with less product loss along the way. When you cut off days or even weeks from the trip from Africa to the slave auction, you greatly increased the survival rate and increased your profits.

If you look at pictures of slave ships of the period, you see that they packed the highest numbers possible into the holds of the ships. The ship's crew would have been greatly outnumbered by the slaves they were transporting. To maintain control, they usually chained them as they lay on their side, head to toe, below decks. They had to lay in their own filth, with very little food or ventilation. They were rarely brought on deck for exercise and fresh air.

To keep costs low, they were usually given barely enough food and water to survive on. Many didn't survive the ordeal. Every cost cutting method they could think of was employed by the slave traders to increase the value of their cargo. If you were talking about anything but the transportation of humans, you would congratulate the Yankee traders on their initiative and creativity."

At this point the alien told me something that I had never heard before. He said, "Slavery was actually a very natural thing. It has existed ever since there were two tribes, once one gained mastery over the other."

He continued. Every great civilization in history was built on the backs of slaves. Rome, Carthage, Egypt, and even the United States probably would not have existed without the benefits of slavery. The industrial revolution, which was influenced by making yet more adjustments to the human brain, gave us the leisure time required to question the moral value of slavery. The creation of machines to do a lot of the labor that slaves had always accomplished did more to end slavery than any moral considerations. It's funny how, the less you personally need slavery, the more morally repugnant it becomes to you.

The alien's comments made me realize that's kind of what happened in the United States, eventually resulting in the Civil War. I know that the winners always write the history but it has always chafed that the revisionists want to say that the Civil War was only about slavery.

Fact is, in the northern states, they found it was cheaper to use "wage slaves" than to actually own a person. Take a look at the child labor abuses, the sweat shops, and the abuses of immigrant laborers in the north. Look at England and how they were involved in the slave trade for years. They used slaves in their colonies but not so much in England itself. They mostly used indentured servants and wage slaves.

Have you ever heard of press gangs? The War of 1812 was triggered by the English practice of taking people from American ships by force and making them serve as seamen in the English Navy. Without the press gangs, the English Navy could not have manned their ships. They did not have a draft system. They simply kidnapped anyone they could find during a press raid and forced them into naval service. They didn't press the upper classes of course. If you didn't come along peacefully, they just knocked you over the head and when you woke up, you would be out at sea. If you didn't do what you were told, you were whipped or worse. Many of the pressed men never saw home again after the bad luck of being swept up in the press. The rigid social system in England kept the lower classes in bondage to the upper classes.

Once again the expanded mental capacity the aliens gave me had me running off at the mouth. I was dredging up material that I had obviously read sometime in my life but was not really aware of on a conscious level.

The use of penal colonies was really another form of slavery. Many of the southern colonies began as penal colonies. Of course, Australia is the most famous penal colony of all. Eventually, as their value to England decreased, and with time to think about it, they decided that slavery was morally wrong and thought it should be stopped world-wide.

The situation reminds me of a story that one of the former Governors of Alabama, Don Siegleman once told. It's a story about taxes but the idea translates to people's feelings about slavery. He was speaking in a small town during his election campaign. He understood that letting the people know you are against sin and other vice is great election fodder so he said: "The first thing I'm going to do is introduce a sin tax!" "Hallelujah!" cried a little old lady near the front. "I'm going to put a new tax on Liquor!" said the Governor. "Amen, Brother Don!" yelled the godly woman. "I'm going to put a new tax on beer!" "Bless him Jesus!" she shouted. Caught up in the spirit of the moment the Governor finished with: "I'm going to put a tax on tobacco products, including snuff!" "Now wait a damned minute! Snuff costs enough already!" screamed the highly perturbed, snuff dipping old woman. The take-away from that is that the only taxes people are for, is the "other people tax." That means any tax is OK as long as it applies to other people but not to you!

Slavery is kind of like that. If it had value to you, then you were accepting of it. You took the good with the bad. If it had no value to you, then you were quick to see the immorality of it all. Thus it was for the North. Since they had already wrung out all the benefits of slavery long ago, and they had time on

59

their hands to think about it, over a period of years of consideration, it became morally repugnant to them.

The alien took over the lecture at this point. It was mostly Northern owned ships that brought the slaves. That was outlawed in 1808 when Congress banned further imports. After that, any new slaves would have to be descendants of those currently in the United States. However, the internal American slave trade and the involvement in the international slave trade or the outfitting of ships for that trade by U.S. citizens were not banned. You could grow your own slaves and sell them. You just could not import any more into the United States. You could also still engage in the slave trade anywhere else in the world where it was legal. Though there were certainly violations of this law, slavery in America became, more or less, self-sustaining.

The biggest change this caused was that slave owners purchased more women. Before this, they purchased mostly males. When they were forced to grow their own slaves, they began to purchase almost as many women as men. This of course, led to increased fornication between master and slave. At first the law said that if the father of a mixed race child was not a slave, then the child was free. That loophole was soon changed so that the status of the mother dictated whether the mixed race child was free or slave.

Over the years, this led to a caste system being established within the slave quarters. The lighter skinned slaves were perceived as smarter, better looking, more valuable, and most likely to get the higher skilled jobs. The darker skinned slaves were field hands for the most part. This perception still exists among the black community today.

I remembered reading about the scandalous actions of Thomas Jefferson (scandalous if viewed by modern eyes) so I commented. A highly visible example of the intermingling of bloodlines between master and slave is represented by the family of Thomas Jefferson. He had a relationship for years with a slave woman who was actually the half sister of his deceased wife. Even though they had several children, Thomas Jefferson never freed his slaves during his lifetime.

The alien continued. The anti-slavery morality movement started with the Quakers – who never had slaves nor traded in slaves to start with. The wholesale removal of the property of others wouldn't affect them at all. Freeing the slaves would have been an 'other people's tax.' It didn't help Northern feelings that the Southern states were so rich because of slavery supported agriculture. It was just too cold in the North for the huge plantations of the South, and cotton doesn't grow well there.

The aliens were amazed that we actually fought a war, supposedly over slavery. As the country grew more industrialized, and machines were invented that took the place of slaves in large scale farming, the institution of slavery would have lost its utility and gone away. When it is useful, it exists. It goes away when it is not. As the aliens noted before, slavery is a natural state in the affairs of humans. There have been and probably will be again, situations where slavery is useful to support the growth of one specific people over another. Just take a look at history. Rome, Egypt, China, Greece, Persia and all the other great civilizations of the past were built by slave labor. Without slavery, humans would still be living in small, isolated villages spread across the planet.

61

By this time I was getting hungry and a little tired of cookies and milk. I asked Elroy if there was anything else to eat.

He replied: "We can make your nutritional materials in any form or flavor you wish."

What I really wanted was a big juicy steak with some fried onions and a baked potato so that's what I said. I wasn't really sure what the aliens ate and I was a little afraid that the idea of eating meat might offend them. Based on years of reading science fiction, I figured the aliens would be evolved to the point where they were only interested in pure nutrition.

Elroy gave me one of his signature laughs and said: "We enjoy a good steak as much as anybody. We just don't get the chance to eat them very often. How about we all go down to the galley and have some steak!"

I was shocked yet pleasantly surprised. The whole group of aliens was twittering happily to each other as we walked down the corridor to the space version of a mess hall where we all enjoyed some of the best steak I ever tasted.

CHAPTER TWELVE

Political Correctness

After eating we walked back to the original work area and the discussion continued. What really amazed the aliens the most was the tremendous amount of political correctness, more easily identified as guilt, generated by the United States period of slavery. How many years must American's pay for the perceived sins of their ancestors? My expanded mental capacity again clicked in and I began my discourse on the subject.

You have to judge whether an action or institution is acceptable based on the time period in which it occurred. Judging the actions of people 200 to 300 years ago by the standards of today is silly and downright counter-productive. No one living today had anything to do with slavery. If you feel America owes you something because your ancestors came here as slaves, then you are wrong. This is the land of the free. You are free to move around within America to seek greater opportunities and you are free to leave America if you want to.

On the western coast of equatorial Africa you find the tiny country of Liberia. Beginning in 1820, the region was colonized by freed American slaves who had the help of the anti-slavery movement in America. They believed ex-slaves would have greater freedom and equality if they returned to Africa. They also did not want all those freed slaves living in their neighborhood. So they took the high road and established them their own country in Africa. Slaves freed from slave ships were also sent there instead of being sent back to their countries of origin. In 1847, the freed slaves founded the Republic of Liberia, establishing a government modeled on that of the United States. They named the capital city Monrovia after the fifth president of the United States (President Monroe) who was a prominent supporter of the colonization of Liberia.

The colonists monopolized the political and economic sectors of the country despite comprising only a small percentage of the indigenous population. They used the knowledge and skills they developed while in America to rule over the more primitive locals. Even though a lot of people in America said they supported freedom from slavery, they really didn't care what the ex-slaves did as long as they did it somewhere else.

A lot of people use their interpretation of the Constitution as an excuse for all kinds of weirdness. I agree with the aliens who supported the creation of the idea of the United States. They quietly encouraged the writers of the greatest living document of government that has ever been achieved in human existence, the Constitution.

It established that equal opportunities for success will be available for all citizens. The key word is "opportunities." The talent and drive of the individual will dictate the success or failure of the individual to achieve success. There is no guarantee of success. The only guarantee is that you have the opportunity to go as far as your natural talent takes you. They did not intend that selected groups of individuals would have preferential treatment because of where they came from.

A lot of African-Americans' ancestors came here as slaves, but not all of them. Even though there were ten to twelve million slaves imported into the New World, only between four hundred and fifty to six hundred thousand of them actually came into what became the United States. The rest went to the islands and to South America. Nearly nine hundred thousand people emigrated here from Africa since 1965. At the height of slavery in America, there were less than four million total, most of them born here.

Only about 13,000 freed slaves chose to return to Africa to settle in Liberia. This was a country which was founded specifically for them and where they dominated the indigenous people even though they made up a tiny portion of the total population. A modern liberal would probably think that as ex slaves, they would abhor slavery and would be good leaders. In fact, they lorded over the locals and practiced their own form of slavery.

A lot of Irish people came here because of the dream of better opportunities in America. Between 1820 and 1920 more than 4,400,000 Irish arrived with nothing but their dreams to sustain them. They were initially treated as the lowest social cast upon arrival. The Italians suffered the same fate. From 1899 to 1924 over 3,800,000 Italians arrived on our shores. The Chinese were imported as cheap labor to build railroads, mine the abundant minerals of the west, and they were also treated as the lowest order of human life.

During World War II, Japanese Americans, mostly from the west coast, were rounded up and put in our own version of concentration camps. We called them internment camps so they were OK. After Pearl Harbor we were afraid of every Japanese American and suspected them of being spies or worse. This was a great excuse to get them out of their homes and confiscate their property in the name of the greater good.

It turned out that most Japanese Americans were very patriotic toward America and wanted to serve their new country. The famous 442nd Regimental Combat Team was an all Japanese American unit that distinguished itself in the European Theatre during the war even though most had families in the internment camps back in the USA. The 442nd produced twenty one Medal of Honor winners, justifying their motto "go for broke."

Every wave of immigrants suffered from discriminatory practices when large numbers of them first came to America. Most of them overcame the difficulty by hard work, education, and perseverance. It was not government set-asides and social programs that made them successful. The opportunity to achieve this is the true "American Dream." In today's highly technical world, you must promote the best and the brightest if you want America to succeed. You cannot initiate quotas based on race and sex so that the leadership "reflects the face of America." In a perfect world, you get to lead because you are the best, not because the rules have been manipulated to favor you because of things that happened hundreds of years ago. To outsiders looking in, the current situation is insane. How can you continue to maintain excellence in all things when you have to lower standards to pay for perceived transgressions in the past? These are transgressions only when based on modern standards. At the time the events occurred, they were considered natural and the law of the land.

Now it's been nearly one hundred and fifty years since the euphemistically called "War of Northern Aggression" and Yankees don't understand why Southerners are still pissed off about the war. That is the only war in the history of the United States where America beat an enemy and then pillaged the countryside to the extent that we are still not recovered from it. In every other war, the United States wins, and immediately starts rebuilding the country they just defeated.

Look at Japan and Germany and even modern day Iraq. No matter how bad the actions of the defeated nation during the war, the day after it's over, we start sending them boatloads of money to rebuild. The war crimes of Japan and Germany were horrendous yet we put them back together, better than before. Forcing Japan to start over from scratch gave them an industrial advantage that cost the American auto industry its preeminent position world-wide.

Worse still, we spend thousands of lives fighting wars and when we win, we give everything back. Our country needs oil desperately. We beat Iraq fair and square. They have a lot of oil. As far as history is concerned, no one would think it's wrong if we kept the oil. Yet we are scrupulous in not taking anything from the conquered country without paying for it. We pay first with American lives then with American cash.

Where was this thinking when the North vanquished the Confederacy? They called it the "Reconstruction Period" but it was just an excuse to further punish the South for the temerity of revolt. It took years for them to haul away everything they plundered. The thirteen states of the Confederacy went from being the richest states in America to being the poorest and have been that way ever since.

As far as the aliens are concerned, the long term actions of the United States are just not logical. We are all over the map. While the "Red Menace" (Communism) was the main threat to the American way of life, we backed any government that was anti-communist. We didn't worry that they were dictators or that their record on human rights didn't align with ours. We supported more than one South American dictator because they opposed Castro and the spread of Communism. Once the threat of the spread of Communism diminished we immediately withdrew our support and threw them to the wolves.

We supported the Shah of Iran for more than twenty years because he stabilized the mid-east and he was anti-communist. As time passed, America became more liberal and accepting of communism. We then allowed the Shah to fall from power because of perceived human rights violations. His fall created a new threat of Muslim extremists in the area so we supported a new dictator, Sadaam Hussein in Iraq.

For many years Sadaam Hussein was the strong man that stabilized the region until he got greedy and invaded Kuwait. We might have let him get by with that but Saudi Arabia was the next domino in that region and he could have conquered it in short order. That would have given him the control of too much oil. He could have engaged in economic blackmail against us by threatening to withhold access to those oil reserves. To stop this we basically occupied Saudi Arabia, attacked and defeated the Iraqi's in Kuwait and then gave it all back to the original owners. By the way, we paid for the whole thing as well. The aliens just shook their heads in amazement and wondered how we got to this place.

My head was spinning! Where did all this information come from? The increased mental capacity the aliens gave me seems to have made it possible to remember, collate, and actually use information that I had stored on a subconscious level. Most of the things I was saying came from knowledge gained by being there during Operation Desert Storm and reading every article and book I could find on the subject. Before this, I never put it all together. If America is the best this planet has to offer, is there any hope that the aliens will not push the button for a "do-over?"

CHAPTER THIRTEEN

A Different Kind of Slavery

My head was reeling from the recognition of vast amounts of information stored in my head suddenly being released by the alien augmentation of my brain. One of the aliens took over and started describing what happened after slavery officially died in America.

Slavery finally ended in America in 1865. That's when folks got creative. Most people have never heard of "convict leasing." This was slavery in another form. Basically, the law said that you could be used as a slave as punishment for breaking the law. This led some states to lease the use of convicts as labor. Conditions were much the same as in slavery except that there were very few women. Convicts were rented out to work in the fields, clear land, dig ditches, or any kind of manual labor imaginable. The states thought they were getting a good deal since they often didn't even have to feed the convicts and they generated some revenue. The warden usually kept most of it but enough was passed on to keep higher officials happy. Sometimes, the convicts were just turned over to you for a set period of time to be used any way you wanted. They were your property so you had to house, feed, clothe, and doctor them – plus make sure they didn't escape. In some cases, they were just rented out as day labor and returned to state control each night. Either way, it was not a good deal for the convict.

The good people didn't care. As far as they were concerned, if you were a convict, then anything that happened to you was your fault. If the warden or overseer made a few bucks from renting out his convicts, then that was viewed as just and right. After all, they wanted the convicts to be severely punished for whatever heinous act they were incarcerated for. This practice was only stopped after it was pointed out that convict labor cost jobs that free men should have. If it wasn't for this, the program would probably still be going on.

One of the programs used today to transition inmates back into society is called work release. During work release, an inmate lives at a minimum security facility and is delivered to work and picked up each day by a prison van. A portion of the inmate's wages is kept by the prison system to help cover the cost of the program. The rest of the inmate's wages were held in an account to be given to the inmate upon his release from incarceration. It is a constant battle to keep this program open as free people constantly complain that inmates do not deserve to have jobs that a free person could do. Most of the work release jobs are the lowest level jobs that most free people don't want but that is immaterial to those who bash the program. They would rather an inmate be returned to society penniless, with no job skills, with a cold turkey re-introduction to life outside the walls of prison. That maintains a set of circumstances that practically guarantees higher recidivism rates.

At this point I had to interrupt and ask how they knew so much of the details of life on earth. Their answer was simple. They routinely abduct humans and record everything in their minds. They also disguise themselves as humans and walk among us. This made me think of all the History Channel programs on alien abduction, lost time, and claims of aliens among us. The aliens told me that this is part of their disinformation program to lull the humans into complacency. By presenting the truth in a way that invites skepticism, they convert truth to fantasy and fantasy to truth. Ingenious!

The alien continued. Until you get involved with the law, you don't realize how many different ways you can end up in jail. Most people never believe it until it happens to them or someone in their family. Don't get me wrong. Most people in jail belong there. However, in some cases there might be a better way to handle the situation. The first question you have to ask yourself is "do I want to rehabilitate a person or do I want to simply punish a person?" If you rehabilitate a person, they may not go back to jail. If you simply punish a person, the odds are that they will be back in jail regularly and often. Which approach serves society best?

Another offshoot of the abolition of slavery was the concept of the "sharecropper." This bound poor black and white farmers to the richer property owners about as effectively as slavery. The sharecropper worked someone else's land, gave them most of the crops produced, and eked out a meager living if every member of the sharecroppers family worked hard every day. Usually, the property owner would provide the seed, fertilizer, farm tools, and basic food necessities to the sharecropper during the year. Once the crops were harvested, the sharecropper usually found out there was little or nothing left over after these debts were paid. In many cases, the sharecropper would get further and further behind and could not leave the situation they found themselves in."

This was all so depressing that I asked the aliens to talk about some other part of the world for awhile. "No problem," they said.

Elroy suggested we take a break and go on a little trip. I admit I was getting a little bored by the historical lectures and gladly accepted. In no time we were back in the control room. The earth looked like a beautiful blue ball from this far out in space. Elroy manipulated some controls and I felt a little funny. The feeling is a lot like when you go over a smooth bump in the road and get a momentary feeling of weightlessness in the pit of your stomach only more so. The view immediately changed from the beautiful blue earth to a dusty red planet with two moons circling it. I recognized it as Mars.

When I was young and a die-hard science fiction fan, the dream of traveling to Mars was as real as a Christian's desire to go to heaven. While I was incredibly happy to be here I wondered what the significance of Mars was to the issue at hand. Elroy answered the unasked question.

We aliens seeded Mars with intelligent life before they started the experiment on earth.

We didn't watch them very closely and the Martians almost got out of hand. They got so advanced that they actually posed a threat to us who planted them there. Instead of starting over, we had no choice but to sterilize the planet. Not only was all life destroyed, the atmosphere was largely blasted from the planet and most of the water was removed. This insured that the Martian life forms could never accidentally reemerge and threaten our way of life.

This revelation really got my attention. These guys play for keeps. They have the power to end human civilization, as we know it. They can make humans start over from a subsistence level hunter gatherer lifestyle or even worse. They can sterilize the planet and move on. From this point on I plan to pay careful attention to everything they say. That's the only way that I can even hope to find a reason to allow us humans to continue.

After we returned from the short trip to Mars, Elroy told another of the aliens to take over the lecture. I paid more attention than ever before.

CHAPTER FOURTEEN

The World in the 20th Century

If you look at the History Channel or programs on the Discovery Channel, you will see lots of programs about aliens and how they could have affected human history. One of the latest programs details the possibility that aliens helped the Third Reich before and during World War II. This made me ask the aliens point blank: "Did you help the Germans make such tremendous scientific strides during the last century?"

Of course the answer was yes. They saw the tremendous possibilities offered by having one world government. If they could assist a little and achieve a few hundred years of world peace, it could be a good thing to study. If you check back, the closest thing to world peace was the 207 years of the "Pax Romana" (Latin for Roman peace) from 27 BC to 180 AD. In the aliens view, it was time for a new study of the effects of long term peace. Obviously, this did not work out like they hoped it would.

During the early part of the twentieth century, things weren't going well in America. Speculators had ruined the economy and America and the world were mired in the Great Depression. In Germany, they blamed it all on the Treaty of Versailles that ended World War I. Inflation was so high that the currency was no good. They say it took a wheel barrel full of Deutsch marks just to buy a loaf of bread. The punitive nature of the treaty terms embittered the German populace. The aliens stepped in and gave the brain of Adolf Hitler a slight adjustment and the course was set. Turns out that even though Adolf had been pretty much a loser up to this point, a slight adjustment was all it took. His skills as an orator, combined with resentment over the treaty at the conclusion of WWI, plus bleak economic conditions allowed this loser to become Dictator of Germany. He at least had a vision for the future of the world. Yes, his plan called for Germany to rule the planet, but his ultimate vision was for a utopian world with peace lasting for millennia.

Much has been written about where he went wrong. He may or may not have had a drug problem. He may or may not have had syphilis. He may or may not have been unduly influenced by psychics. No one knows for sure. As I said before, the winners write the history. Hitler has been demonized to the extent that if you point out anything good he did, you will be ostracized and ridiculed. That is one of the unintended consequences of political correctness. If you look deep enough, there are some good things about everyone. If you violate even one of the planks of political correctness, all that is cancelled out. It's a good thing the aliens are saying most of these things. I'd probably be run out of town if I had made these observations.

Hitler certainly surrounded himself with a group of self serving thugs who stroked his ego while lining their pockets and improving their position. In spite of the infighting among his underlings, with Hitler's leadership, German forces and their European allies at one point occupied most of Europe and North Africa. You could say that the beginning of the end began with the invasion of Russia.

Early treaties between Germany and Russia were established so that Germany could concentrate on defeating the rest of Europe. Hitler became overconfident and directed the Russian invasion before he had consolidated his earlier gains. A look at history should have told him this was a mistake. Napoleon Bonaparte is considered one of the greatest generals of all time and he failed to conquer the vast territory of Russia. You might be able to defeat the Russian Army but the Russian winter is a terrible thing.

That is why a clear understanding of history is so important. Humans seem to make the same mistakes over and over. If they knew history and learned from past mistakes, a lot of turmoil could be avoided. The failed invasion of Russia significantly contributed to German disaster in 1944, when the Allied armies freed German-occupied Europe.

Hitler's reign resulted in the systematic murder of as many as seventeen million civilians. This includes an estimated six million Jews targeted in the Holocaust and between five hundred thousand and one and a half million Gypsies. Less obvious and nearly always overlooked, he gave us the Volkswagen, the Autobahn, and caused the end of the Great Depression. The political correctness police will slaver at the jaws and gnash their teeth over the last one but it is a fact that World War II ended the Great Depression. Without Hitler, there would have been no World War II.

Another contribution from Nazi Germany was the creation of the foundation for the exploration of space. Many people do not realize that the United States government brought all the German scientists they could get their hands on to

Redstone Arsenal in Huntsville, Alabama. That is where they created the American space program. The Soviet Union collected some as well. Their captured German scientists competed with ours and were the driving force behind the space race. They had many other technological leaps that put them years ahead of the rest of the world but what did you expect? The aliens just made an adjustment here, planted an idea there, and that's all it took. They didn't have to fly to Germany and deliver them a space ship or a set of plans to copy. The ever evolving mind of man is capable of great things. Sometimes it just takes a little nudge.

The whole German thing didn't work out for the aliens so they tried the Communist idea. Pure Communism should be a beautiful thing. Everybody gets what they need. People do things they are good at. Everyone is equal. Sounds great but in practice the human element creeps in. No matter what the group is, there will always be an elite element that thinks it deserves more than everyone else.

In America, we have developed such an entitlement society that almost everyone believes that they are elite and deserve more than everyone else. One of the biggest ideas involved with the Communist doctrine was that religion is bad. They theorized that it was engineered to keep people meek and in their place. Sounds a little familiar doesn't it? Separating people from their religion can be tough. The Russian Communists killed millions of their own people while trying to weed out people that didn't recognize how good Communism would be for them. As the idea spread into China, the same thing happened. Many people just couldn't understand how good pure Communism would be for them and tried to resist. As the Borg said, "Resistance is futile."

For a number of years, Communism spread around the world. It looked like there would be an ultimate ideological clash of the titans between America representing capitalism and the godless Communist countries. As time passed, most of the Communist ruled countries in the world have drifted towards Capitalism while the capitalism based United States is drifting towards socialism (a step on the path to Communism).

Communism is not natural. The concept of taking from each according to their abilities and giving to each according to their needs is not natural. Capitalism is a nature based idea. Some people want more, and are willing to risk their own assets and work harder than most other people to achieve success. This represents selection of the fittest. This is the very foundation of evolution. Modern attempts to go against nature will result in the downward spiral of any country that supports the political correctness initiatives of the modern liberal.

Another of the aliens took over the lecture at this point. It seems that they are each experts in different segments of human history. The thought crossed my mind that with the almost shared consciousness these guys seemed to possess, any of them could have given the whole lecture even though it had already lasted days with no end in sight.

Elroy answered my unasked question. My assumption is correct. They are sharing the lecture duties so that they appear more human to me. The lecture continued.

CHAPTER FIFTEEN

Unintended Results of Political Correctness

There is just no way around it. Sometimes what seems like a good idea at the time ends up a nightmare? At one time, banks and lending institutions in America were allowed to make loans based on your ability to repay the loan. They required a substantial down payment because that made you a part owner from the start. Ownership would encourage you to complete the promised transaction and repay the loan.

Some bleeding hearts noticed that a lot of minorities were not qualifying for home loans. Either they had poor credit, no money for a down payment, or their jobs just would not meet the means test to support repayment of a loan. The PC police exerted political pressure to force the evil bankers to make loans to these poor folks. After all, part of the American Dream is home ownership. These people deserve to own homes just like the people who have good credit; good jobs; and saved up a down payment. It could only be racism if they were not given loans. In today's world of political correctness, no one wants to be labeled racist. That is the ultimate insult.

As you may have guessed, political correctness caused the lenders to make loans that were not supported by the facts. Low income people, many from minority households, could suddenly purchase a home with no money down. A lot of these loans went bad from the start. The lenders wanted to charge them higher interest rates because they were a higher risk for non-payment. Absolutely not, shouted the PC police. That would be racism. A whole industry sprang up that catered to the home financing needs of poor and minority households. They would secure an inflated appraisal that supported any amount needed to make the loan. The long term expectation was that the ever increasing value of the mortgaged property would eventually cover the value of the loan even if it didn't to start with. When the housing bubble burst, we all found out that was not true.

Other than inflated home values and unsecured loans, the world was a wonderful place. The great unwashed could own homes just like the working class. Liberals were ecstatic. Then, the unintended consequence reared its head. Since these folks had no money invested in their new homes, it was much like paying rent to them. If they got behind on their payments, they just walked away. They never paid much attention to the concept that you gave your word that you would pay the mortgage. If it was inconvenient to make a payment, it was all right in their minds not to do so. This flooded the market with repossessed homes. More homes on the market made the price of homes fall. Falling prices meant more home buyers had upside down mortgages where they owed more than the house was worth. This made more people walk away from their promise to pay.

Can you guess what the PC police said then? They accused the lenders they strong armed into making mortgage loans to the unqualified of racism! That's right! Since banks and mortgage companies set up programs to help minorities achieve home ownership, they were obviously racist. They knew all along that this was a high risk group of borrowers and yet they still made the loans. What's a little political pressure got to do with it? The repercussions of this are still being felt. Home construction is down, it's harder to get a mortgage again, fortunes were lost, banks closed, retirement funds went broke and a whole lot more. All influenced by good intentions.

There are all kinds of touchy feely programs that go against nature yet are embraced by some vocal group of Americans. They all have unintended consequences.

Let's talk about wild horses. There were no horses in America until the Spanish invasion brought them here. Over a period of time, many horses escaped into the wild, where they adapted and established thriving herds. Most people don't realize it but humans all over the planet have been eating horse meat as long as there have been horses. In the Viking culture, eating horse meat was a part of their religion.

Scroll forward to today where you find vast herds of wild horses running loose all over the American West. Because of the movies and television, horses are given credit for being a lot smarter than they really are. They are seen as part of the fabric and history of America. Anyone who mentions eating a horse is looked on as if they were a cannibal. Our ancestors ate horse meat and just about any other kind of meat that was available. Other parts of the world still eat horse meat. With all these wild horses running loose, plus all the unwanted pet horses available across America, there were actually two slaughter houses in America that killed and processed horse meat for worldwide distribution for human consumption.

When the do-gooders found out, they shrilly demanded that this abomination be stopped at once. Who wants to think about the lovely horse being butchered for food? They are practically a part of the family! Finally, the last two horse meat processing plants were closed. Hurrah for the PC police! They solved another problem that the rest of us mouth breathing retards didn't even know existed.

What unintended consequence did this generate? First, everyone employed in the two plants lost their jobs then everyone that depended on the trickle down income from their spending also suffered. The plants were reopened across the border in Mexico and Canada. They got our jobs.

With no legal horse processing plant available, the horse herds continued to grow beyond the lands ability to sustain them. They overgrazed existing open range land, destroying it and denying its use for growing cattle. The cost of raising cattle for human consumption went up. The government was finally forced to step in and feed the wild horses. Because of the cost of feeding horses they can't sell and have no use for, they are considering killing thousands of horses. Remember, they will be killed and buried but not made available as food for the starving people of the world. What started out as a good idea just gets worse and worse.

Think about mainstreaming. There was a time in America when what were called retarded children (a medical term of that period, now called "special" children, were kept at home, out of sight. As industrialization gave us more time on our hands, it gave us time to consider more abstract ideas. We were no longer concerned with just getting enough to eat, a warm shelter and so on. We started wondering whether things were "right."

As always, the squeaky wheel gets the grease so a movement was started that advanced the rights of the mentally challenged to live just like normal folks. What everyone forgot is this. They are not normal. For years special classes were established where the mentally challenged could pretend they were normal and go to school every day. They would learn to go to the bathroom by themselves, finger paint, and so on. This also gave the parents a break from taking care of these "special" people.

As years passed, some other squeaky wheel types decided that this was not enough. They had to develop a suitable curriculum to teach these special children things that normal kids were taught. Once again, the problem is that they are not normal. More time passed, and with all this time on their hands to think about things like this, it was demanded that these "special" children should be allowed to mainstream with other students. Exposure to normal children was to have a positive effect on their success in learning to live in a normal world.

Reality rears its ugly head here. Instead of making it better for the "special" children, it made it worse for the normal children whose learning was held back by the extra time spent by teachers catering to the needs of the "special" children. Although it started as a beautiful thought, it ended up holding back the learning of thousands of otherwise normal children.

One of the utopian dreams of all liberals is the Head Start Program. It was going to lift up the poor and downtrodden by giving them more public schooling at an earlier age. This would include free breakfast and lunch so that the parent's failure to provide for their children's nutritional needs would not hold them back. The program assumes the responsibility of the parent for providing adequate meals for the children enrolled in the program. After spending billions of dollars and years of effort, the Head Start Program is a resounding flop. It's only practical value is as state paid day care. Most children enrolled in Head Start do no better in school than the children who stay home with their family until elementary school starts. The parents benefit from the free day care and the children are assured of at least two decent meals per day. If that was the original intention then we would have a resounding success on our hands. Alas, that was not part of the plan.

During my entire life I had never thought about most of the things the aliens were talking about. Could we humans have really screwed up so many things by accident? It was worth some thought.

I asked Elroy if we could take another break for food and a nap. I wasn't as tired as I would have been before the aliens tuned up my mind and body. I really just wanted a break from the litany of mankind's failures. To hear about it all at once from such an authoritative source was almost too much to take. The aliens have had us under close scrutiny since the first ape man wandered across the African plains millions of years ago. If anyone knows about our successes and failures, it would be them.

Once I was alone, I took another one of those refreshing waterless showers, had a snack, and laid down for some contemplation. It wasn't long before I was fast asleep.

When I woke up I immediately noticed that I felt even better than ever. It seems that each time I sleep the aliens do a little more work. Since no one was around I decided to perform a little experiment.

I started with doing some pushups. Just the normal kind like we did years ago in the Army. After I had done 100 of them without getting tired I stopped and started doing sit-ups. Again, I stopped at 100. Not only was I not tired, I wasn't even breathing hard. If I could bottle this or put it in a pill form, I could make a fortune back on earth. There were no weights around so I walked over to my Harley. I stood behind it and grabbed one rear shock in each hand. With almost no effort I was able to lift the back tire about a foot off the ground. I was so surprised that I almost dropped it.

About this time the whole group of aliens came back into the room. Apparently they had watched the entire range of my physical exertions on a view screen in another room. Elroy asked me if I was pleased with the work they had done.

"Oh yeh! I've never been this strong or felt this great!"

"Glad you like it," said Elroy. "Let's get on with the story. I'm getting pressure to make a decision about earth and want to cover everything with you and get your insight before I make it."

CHAPTER SIXTEEN

Forced Busing, or How to Screw Up the School System

The shortest alien began his lecture. Let's take a look at the issue of forced busing. An unintended consequence was that it killed the neighborhood school. A primary catalyst for the development of forced busing was an influential report on educational equality commissioned by the U.S. government in the 1960s. The result was a massive report of over seven hundred pages. That report written in 1966 contained many controversial findings.

Conclusions from the study revealed that black schools in the South were not significantly underfunded as compared to white schools and per-pupil funding did not contribute significantly to differences in educational outcomes. Despite this they decided that socially disadvantaged black children would still benefit significantly from learning in mixed-race classrooms. Thus, it was argued that busing was necessary for achieving racial equality.

Based on the findings they decided that you could not simply increase funding to segregated schools to make them equal. This really stirred up the liberals because they wanted to believe that black schools got less money and that was a major reason for lack of achievement by their students. This study showed that was not the case but the liberals went charging ahead anyway.

A famous brief written by Chief Justice Earl Warren claimed that segregation is psychologically harmful to black children and implied that all-black classrooms are inherently inferior. Warren's ambiguous opinion allowed lower courts and lawmakers to infer that stopping segregation was not enough, but that social justice depended upon integrating the races in school, at whatever cost to neighborhoods and to children, black and white.

Armed with this information and driven by a desire to redress past wrongs, it was determined that forced mingling of the races in public schools through forced busing would result in a redistribution of school funding and would correct years of neglect and liberal perceptions of lower economic support for African-American schools. This redistribution of funding would elevate the students from the poor African-American schools. The do-gooders also felt attending school with their affluent white neighbors would elevate the achievement of less affluent minority students.

Everyone knows this was not the result. Instead of elevating the intended student target, it lowered the achievements of the other students. It actually achieved similar results as mainstreaming. Neighborhood schools were just that, neighborhood schools. An affluent neighborhood had an affluent school. A poor neighborhood had a less affluent school.

A more important consideration should have been the feeling that originally, the school belonged to the families in the community. More families participated in school programs when they felt ownership as they did with neighborhood schools. More parental support was given to teachers within their neighborhood schools. In fact, many of the long term teachers taught more than one generation and in some cases, as many as three generations of students from the same family. That gives neighborhood families a sense of ownership and belonging.

The loss of neighborhood schools in the African-American community meant a loss of connection to their school. Parents had no connection to the white school their kids had to go to and felt little need to participate.

Run the clock forward a few decades and see the shambles of the American education system. Neighborhood schools were destroyed. Established traditions bit the dust when schools were combined to achieve racial parity. Inner city schools went from segregated to mixed, then back to mostly segregated again.

White flight to the suburbs and creation of "Christian Schools" reduced the numbers of white students available to balance out the minority population in the inner city schools.

It's kind of interesting that "Christian School" has become the code name for mostly white schools. No one set out to destroy the American education system. It was an unintended consequence of knee jerk reactions to perceived inequities within the system. Rather than face them and address them with a well thought out plan, they just took the path of least resistance without a thought to future results.

Another, less obvious aspect of forced busing was the continued punishment of the Southern states. Since the Civil War, the north never misses a chance to pretend social superiority over the southern states.

89

Most northern states are in total denial concerning their treatment of minorities. They historically treated each wave of immigrants as less than human yet were fixated on the Southern states treatment of the freed slaves and their ancestors. This may have occurred because it was easier to spot the darker skinned citizens than the pale skinned Jews, Irish, Italians, and so on. Skin colors made it easier to spot discriminatory practices and denounce them.

Most of the Southern states were made to endure forced busing long before it was instituted in the north. In Massachusetts, where the liberal Kennedys were from, there were massive riots when Boston schools were required to participate in forced busing in 1974. There was no national outcry over this. If something similar had happened in the South, federal troops would have been called out.

Robert Nisbet wrote in The *Quest for Community* that the central crisis of the 20th century is the continuous assault on "natural authority" and the feeling of community, through the state's (meaning federal government's) progressive invasion into our daily lives. The alleged disorganization of the modern family is, in fact, simply an erosion of its natural authority, the consequence, in considerable part, of the absorption of its functions by other bodies, chiefly the state. Busing is a perfect example of such a state-sponsored assault on community and family.

By 1998, Boston public-school enrollment dropped from 93,000 to 57,000 and the proportion of white students shrank from sixty five percent of total enrollment to twenty eight percent. Seventy-eight school buildings closed their doors. At that time, whites made up seventeen percent of public-school students. Most white students attended one of the three private schools, like the Boston Latin School. Boston was forced to lower its official threshold for the acceptable racial balance of each school from a minimum of fifty percent white in 1965 to a minimum of nine percent.

Busing has not only failed to integrate Boston schools, it also failed to improve education opportunities for the city's black children. When Boston introduced Stanford 9 testing to the public schools in 1996, over ninety percent of seventh-graders at Woodrow Wilson Elementary School scored "poor" or "failing" in math, as did seventy three percent of fifth-graders at Brighton's Alexander Hamilton School. At Dorchester's William E. Endicott School, ninety five percent of the fifth-graders scored "poor" or "failing" in reading and one hundred percent scored "poor" or "failing" in math. Yet all of these students were promoted to the next grade.

After absorbing so many facts in such a short period of time I was ready for a change of scenery. I asked Elroy if there had ever been life on any other planets in our solar system.

He replied: "Let's take a short trip to the moons of Jupiter and I will show you."

We all trooped back to the forward control room and within moments we were there. Up close, Jupiter is beautiful and seems to fill the whole sky. Ganymede, Europa, and Callisto are three of the sixty seven recognized moons of Jupiter. Ganymede is actually larger than the planet Mercury. Europa and Callisto are both bigger than ex-planet Pluto. Earth scientists believe that these three moons may have what it takes to support life, as we know it. The requirements are liquid water, you need a source of heat, you need stability over time and you need organic compounds. The European Space Agency is planning to investigate the possibility of life on

Jupiter, with its Jupiter Icy moons Explorer (JUICE) mission set to investigate three of Jupiter's moons in a mission that will start in 2022. Meanwhile, NASA continues to dedicate its resources to Mars.

"It's all very beautiful but the question remains, is there life on these moons?"

Elroy's initial response was a chuckle. "While the surface of these moons may look bleak, it's what's inside that counts. That's all I can say about that."

With that, we returned to our Earth orbit and the historical review continued.

CHAPTER SEVENTEEN

Let's Screw Up the School System Even More

The vaunted program "No Child Left Behind" established an array of standardized tests that evaluate progress through the school system. Your job as a teacher depended on achieving certain scores on the tests. If improvements were shown you could even receive a financial bonus. Federal dollars were attached to test scores. If you showed improvement, then your school system was eligible to receive extra money. That way, not only the teachers but the school administrators and even the school system could benefit by improving test scores. Think about it. They included measurable standards so they could insure accountability. The objective was to give every child the same opportunities since they all had to compete on the same standardized tests. What were the results?

Most of a teachers time is now spent teaching the test. There is no room for expanding the mind through exploring new ideas and developing original thought. You have to stick to the curriculum that feeds improved test results. Widespread cheating by the faculty was another result. Most weeks you can read about another school system either being praised for making improvements or being investigated for cheating.

93

Some systems are praised and held up as a shining example until a closer look reveals the cheating. The liberal thinkers desperately want programs like this to succeed so they don't look too closely until a third party forces them to.

A grand jury indictment in Atlanta detailed the culture of adult cheating that existed in Atlanta public schools during the tenure of a recently disgraced superintendent. She was once "Superintendent of the Year" and received about $580,000 in performance bonuses. She fired whistle-blowers and protected the jobs of those that participated in a massive program to change student's answers to standardized test questions from wrong to right answers.

Is this an isolated case? There is reason to believe that policies tying adult incentives to children's test scores have resulted in a nationwide uptick in cheating. *The Atlanta Journal Constitution* investigated and found 196 school districts across the country with suspicious test score gains similar to the ones demonstrated in Atlanta. Statisticians said there was only a one in one billion likelihood of the test score gains being legitimate. A 2011 study by *USA Today* of test scores from six states found 1,610 instances in which gains were as likely to be legitimate as you are likely to win the lottery. Until we conduct independent, local investigations nationwide, we simply cannot know the full extent of the cheating. This makes it impossible to determine whether the United States ought to continue to link teacher and administrator pay and job security to kids' standardized test scores.

What's wrong with giving certain groups special consideration? It is unnatural. In nature, only the Alpha male gets to mate. The biggest and fastest survive while the slower, smaller, and dumber don't do so well. That supports evolution and improvement of the species. The best and brightest succeed while the rest take their place in society based on their individual abilities. That is at it should be.

America has turned its back on this most basic concept. The whole societal fixation on providing redress for the sins of the past is totally without merit. Putting in quotas based on sex, race, religion, physical or mental handicaps, or anything other than the ability of the individual is unnatural, uncalled for, and un-American.

After hearing the aliens view on our politically correct social programs, I could see why they supported the ancient Romans and the Nazi's. The alien's view seemed to be that logic should prevail over emotion and sentimentality and that seems to be what the aliens want from us humans. We humans do not make decisions simply based on logic. That is part of what makes us human. Maybe most of our social programs did turn out to yield different results than we thought they would. In spite of the results, we were trying to make things better. It just didn't always work.

I asked Elroy if they have ever started over on the earth project in the past.

"Of course we have. Sometimes we just have to clean up a certain geographical area but sometimes it is necessary to wipe the slate clean and begin again."

"Can you be a little more specific?" I asked.

In the area you call India we destroyed some cities containing people who had drifted too far off the path we wanted them to take. They were all in the area around Mohendjo Daro and Harapa. There are still traces of radioactivity there from that cleansing. Sometimes we make it look like natural phenomenon causing the destruction. Almost all your ancient civilizations have legends of devastating floods wiping out most of humanity. Didn't you ever wonder why? Sometimes we just change the weather for a few centuries and that pretty much wipes the slate clean.

I didn't answer but my thoughts were all over the map. Could the biblical story of Saddam and Gomorrah be an example of an alien start-over? Were the Ice Ages caused by the aliens instead of just being a natural phenomenon? Was there really an Atlantis that influenced cultures all over the world before disappearing under the waves? While I really wanted to know the answers, I was afraid to ask. What if the aliens caused these disasters?

CHAPTER EIGHTEEN

What Is Different About Me?

My mind was reeling. I needed a break from hearing about how bad things were in the country I loved, so I tried to steer the conversation back to a safer subject. The aliens told me earlier that my DNA was closer to the desired outcome of their experiment than anyone else. This intrigued me and obviously led to questions. What is different about me? I have noticed some things about myself that were different from other people but till now I didn't think about just how different I was.

One of the ways that I know I am different is that I think in multiple dimensions while most people think in a "flat" or linear way. I see that any action will result in multiple reactions and not just the one intended. Most people only see their intended result with no thought for the many unintended consequences of their actions.

My IQ has been tested several times over the years and the results range from a score of 137 to 143. The average human scores 100. I never thought of myself as a genius but realized a long time ago that I can see a lot of different possibilities to deal with a situation while most other people see only one or two. Somehow my mind breaks things down into smaller pieces and I am able to make something that seems complex to others into something that seems simple to me. This has caused me a lot of problems over the years trying to explain why I do the things I do. One truth that I have learned is that I am right a lot more often than I am wrong.

Probably the biggest difference in me and other people is that I tend to make a plan and follow it. I do not just drift along from day to day. I don't require instant gratification. I don't have to be the first to buy the latest Apple product or stand in line all night to be the first to see the latest fad film. I can plan to make a purchase and save my money to pay cash rather than charge it and pay principal and interest. I rarely pay retail for anything and I never pay interest. To me it is simple logic to act this way yet I rarely meet another human who does so.

While I have always been aware that I often see things differently than my fellow humans, this was the first time I had an inkling of a possible reason why.

The leader of the aliens communicated with me telepathically. When I understood his communication he followed up with this: "You are advanced enough to be able to communicate with us telepathically. Most humans are not. Don't you remember times in your life when you thought you were different? Were there times when you felt you knew what was going to happen next?"

As I thought about these questions, my mind drifted back to my youth.

My first grade teacher couldn't believe it when I could read almost immediately. There was no reason for it. I did not go to the high speed kindergarten programs that are everywhere today. There was no such thing as Head Start back in those days. One of my earliest memories was the feeling of frustration I felt while listening to the other first graders trying to read, "See Spot run." I just could not understand why they couldn't read as well as I could. My teacher told my mother that I was driven to be the best in everything we did. In other grammar school grades we had math races on the blackboard. I usually won them.

In today's politically correct world, these events would not be allowed as the losers might feel diminished self esteem which could scar them for life. The primary question is this. Was I competitive based on my DNA or did the competitive exercises prevalent in school during those days cause me to be so competitive? Perhaps it is some of both. My alien inspired DNA made me seek competition and the school environment gave me a chance to develop my competitive spirit. All I know is that all my life I just wanted to be the best there ever was in anything that held my interest. If I wasn't interested, I couldn't care less.

Over the years, my motives have been continually called into question. Other people just can't seem to understand that being the best is a reward in and of itself. No money has to change hands to make me feel great. I guess they were just projecting their own values onto my actions. I sometimes feel that they do this because they know that they can't compete with me so they attempt to denigrate my achievements by assigning some form of sinister motivation for my actions. All I know is that my goal is always to be the very best I can be and always do the right thing for the right reason. I may not follow every rule. Especially when the rules are stupid. But I never do a thing that violates the public trust.

I don't want to be able to do everything or think I know everything. My strength has always been that I know where to find someone who can answer any question. I recognize the value of the knowledge provided by experts and listen to them. I know what technicians are for. Again, I don't think I know it all. I just know what I don't know and I know how to apply the knowledge the technicians have in ways they would never think of. It's amazing how many people fail at this simple trait.

In 1970, I was deep in the throes of my first love. It was probably a product of my naiveté, but for many months, I actually turned down the opportunity to have sex with this girl because "I loved her." When I later gave in to my natural urges, and her pleas to take her virginity before she left for college, I did my best to make up for lost time.

We were napping on a pile of U-Haul quilts upstairs in my Father's house. Almost constant and consecutive bouts of love making had us both, more than a little exhausted. Lingering on the edge of sleep, I sat bolt upright on the make shift bed as the vivid image of my best friend wrecking my car leaped into my brain. Of course the names are changed here since I would not want to embarrass anyone so, Caroline asked me, "What was the matter?" I told her that William had just wrecked my car. It was a 4 door station wagon. In my vision I saw the car slide off the road and the door behind the driver caved in from impact against a tree. She said that was ridiculous. William was asleep downstairs and my car was parked outside where I left it.

Since the image seemed so real to me, I got up and looked out the window. My car was gone. I put on pants and ran downstairs. William was gone as well. As I stood there wondering what was going on, William turned in the driveway in my car. There were weeds sticking out of the grill and the passenger door behind the driver was caved in. He "borrowed" the car to practice driving on the curvy, country road near the house. Like many young drivers, he thought he was a much better driver than he was. He entered a curve too fast, slid off the road, spun all the way around, and side swiped a tree.

A check of the time of the accident revealed that the vision came to me at the same time the event occurred. At the time it happened, it was an isolated incident. I thought it was very strange but kept it to myself, as I had nothing else to link it to. As years passed, other visions or examples of precognition manifested themselves. Some examples could be called coincidence. Some could be called the result of experience indicating the possibility of an occurrence.

As years passed, and more and more of these visions appeared, I started to heed them. Many times I have thought of calling someone on the telephone and when I pick it up to dial, they are already on the other end. They were calling me while I was thinking about calling them. Yes, this could be viewed as coincidence. But, how many times must it happen before you are no longer surprised?

Just the other day, driving home near dark, the vision of deer in the road flashed into my consciousness. Because of the number of times that these images are right, I slowed down immediately. Moments later, I saw a deer just off the road to the left in someone's yard. This caused me to slow even more. Just as I looked back at the road, three more deer ran across in front of me. If I had not slowed down, we would have proven that multiple objects cannot occupy the same space at the same time. My small Honda would have suffered terribly from impact with three deer!

Speaking of impact, when I was seventeen years old I had one of the fastest production motorcycles on the planet. It was a Kawasaki 350 Avenger SS which I had ridden at 115 mph with two people on it! It had a two cycle engine with rotary valves. This caused the carburetors to be mounted on the sides of the engine making the engine very wide. The front foot-peg position hid your feet behind the carburetors.

Like most seventeen year olds, I thought I was indestructible and this influenced my riding style. One afternoon I was flying down the road at about eighty five miles per hour when I noticed a car ahead weaving slightly from left to right but mostly staying in his lane. He turned on the right turn signal so I opened up the throttle and swung wide left to pass him at about one hundred and ten miles per hour. With no warning he began to turn left in front of me.

I have to point out that the car was an early model Corvair Monza so what happens next makes sense. When the car started to turn left, my body went on automatic pilot. I locked down the brakes, downshifted, and matched the angle of his turn simultaneously. I hit the side of his car just in front of the rear tire with the covering over the right hand carburetor the only part of the Kawasaki that touched the car. My speed and trajectory allowed me to make a crease down the side of the Corvair all the way to the front bumper. That model Corvair had a flimsy piece of light weight chrome serving as the front bumper. The end of the bumper caught the covering over the carburetor and ripped the whole side off the engine. At the same time, the bumper bent in the middle and stuck straight out in front of the car. The impact with the bumper caused the speed to drop to less than five miles per hour immediately. My hand squeezed the clutch and I rolled to a stop on the side of the road. I looked down at the shattered but still running engine and could see one of the pistons going up and down. I turned off the key and that was it. That was the last time that engine ever ran.

The miracle of this episode was that I hit a car while traveling about one hundred and ten miles per hour on a motorcycle and never even fell down. The motorcycle was destroyed but I didn't even get a scratch. If I had thought about it, there was no way that I could have planned and executed my escape from disaster. Something outside me seemed to take over and the next thing I know, I'm rolling to a stop, safe and sound.

Another way that I have felt "special" in my later years involves "giving." You can call it creating good Karma, God blessing the cheerful giver, or just plain coincidence. I choose to believe that doing good things is what we are here for. I know that I do them for the good feeling it gives me but some higher power is involved and going the extra mile to reward and encourage my behavior.

Not long ago, I gave $250 to a couple of elderly widows so they could visit each other and have some enjoyment in their last years. Afterwards, but in the same week, I was given a $250 bonus at work. Another time I gave $2500 to a poor man in another state who really needed a hand. By the time I got home, I had surprise checks in the mail totally slightly more than $2500. Three checks arrived from unexpected sources and more than covered the amount I gave away. This has happened in my life many times during the past few years. This has to do with a direct connection to a higher power. It's not a reference to any modern human religious practices.

Today, if I feel that I should do something for someone, I just do it. The Indian Shaman "Two Hawks" gives us three rules to live by. Lead by example. Be tolerant of others. Make the world a better place. Was Two Hawks really an alien? I don't know, but based on what I learned during my time on board the spaceship, it could be true. It seems that the way I act towards my fellow man, plus the occasional glimpse into the near future that my brain receives is exactly where the aliens wanted mankind to be at this point in their evolution. Their despair is caused by the fact that there are so few of us who have reached this point. They had hoped that more of us would have developed this far or even further by now.

CHAPTER NINETEEN

We Gave Women the Vote

Now that we had come so far, I asked for more insights from the leader of the alien group. What other examples existed of unintended consequences and their effect on earth's people. Some of the things they said are there right in front of us. We are just so busy living that we don't notice them or make the connection.

One wild example of unintended consequence involved giving women the vote. All the political correctness police will sit up on the edge of their chair for this one. How dare anyone, even aliens, say that giving women the vote wasn't a good thing? The alien leader told me that giving women the vote eventually ruined the American family! Most people blame the invention of television for that but that's another story.

"How can you say that? Please explain this to me."

The aliens all agreed that giving women the vote was a dangerous thing. The first thing they wanted to do was flex their political muscle. Even before being allowed to vote themselves, wrapped in the banner of religious ecstasy, they proceeded to push Prohibition. They were convinced that the demon rum was the ruination of America and American values. The Woman's Christian Temperance Union (WCTU) was founded in 1873. The WCTU advocated the prohibition of alcohol. Frances Willard, of the WCTU, stated the aims of the organization were to create a "union of women from all denominations, for the purpose of educating the young, forming a better public sentiment, reforming the drinking classes, transforming by the power of Divine grace those who are enslaved by alcohol, and removing the dram-shop from our streets by law." Women in general, supported prohibition as a method for preventing the abuses of alcoholic husbands. The women of the WCTU fought to preserve the sanctity of the home by the prohibition of alcohol. Guess what? It didn't work out too well.

The period of Prohibition from 1920 to 1933 was filled with lawlessness and ill gotten gains. The government could make liquor illegal but it could not stop the people from wanting it. Fortunes were made by those who flouted the law and ran speakeasies or were involved in bootlegging. Wars between rival gangs seeking control of the lucrative liquor racket were rampant. Finally, the government had to give up. The majority of the people of America either wanted alcohol or didn't want to force their views on everyone else. That is the major downfall of the self righteous. They always want to force their views on everyone around them. It's not enough that they follow certain moral guidelines. They want everyone else to have to follow them too.

Since Prohibition didn't work out, women set their sights on another male dominated institution. Once prevalent in every town in America, they were given names like the "gentleman's club", "cat house", "house of ill repute" or the more descriptive "whore house." Women really didn't understand their function but thought they did. To women, these sites were pits of degradation where godless acts of abandonment went on. The self righteous thought these were establishments where women were enslaved and reduced to commodities for the lustful entertainment of low class men. This was where alcohol and loose women sucked the life out of the American family.

Nothing could be further from the truth. Sure, there were some low class dives out there that catered to vile, prurient interests but we are speaking of the broader spectrum here. In most cases, the "gentlemen's club" was a place that a man might stop off for a little relaxation after work. He could spend time with other members of his working/social class in a non-threatening atmosphere. They might play a friendly game of cards, make a business deal, talk politics, smoke cigars, or have a drink or two. If they had the urge they could acquire the services of an attractive lady and go upstairs for a few minutes of non-judgmental, no strings attached sexual release.

After spending some time winding down from a day at work, most men went home to their families. They went to church, paid their taxes, and most of them stayed married to the same woman for life. The wife was placed on a pedestal. They wouldn't think of drinking in their home. That would have been an insult to the lady of the house. There are things a man might like to do with a "professional woman" that he would never ask his wife to do. His wife would probably have been shocked and mortified at the suggestion. If she wasn't, then the husband would always wonder about the wife. Where did she learn to do that? She's not supposed to like it, is she? The "gentlemen's club" provided a safe and natural environment for manly activities that are totally natural and have been with us since Adam and Eve ate the apple. That biblical reference was the aliens attempt at humor.

Let's get back to the point. Women weren't having any of this. They banded together and got Prohibition passed even before they had the vote. After they got the vote, they were a self righteous juggernaut! In town after town, women banded together and closed these vile establishments. They were triumphant and reveled in their righteous fury.

What was the unintended consequence? The total destruction of the family unit was the result. Think about it. When these places were legal or at least accepted and overlooked, a man could spend some quality time away from his family in a safe, comfortable environment. Since there was competition and it wasn't illegal, prices were low. The impact on the family was minimal. Most important, a man could have meaningless sex with an attractive woman at low cost. Afterwards, guilt free, he went home to be a wonderful family man. Because he was so relaxed, he probably treated his family better than he would have if he arrived home straight from work, tense and ornery from a hard day on the job.

Women just don't get it. Their question is always, "what does she have that I don't?" It's simply a question of variety. I love apple pie but I don't want to eat it every day. If I sometimes eat a slice of chocolate pie, that doesn't mean I don't still love apple pie. Women just don't get it. Women demanded that these magnificent cultural establishments be closed.

Men now had to go to a bar if they wanted a drink. Bars are there for one purpose. That is to sell you as much alcohol as they can. Any other activities are a distance second. Worse still, the natural man will always crave variety. With these community service establishments closed, they can no longer indulge in meaningless, no strings attached, low cost sex with a

108

stranger. They now have to establish a relationship with a female to have sexual variety. The time and money spent establishing the relationship required to achieve this goal takes away from the family unit. When the relationship is exposed, which they almost always are, the family unit is destroyed.

Let's take a close look at where this slippery slope has taken us. Modern women are now pressing for laws that make a man who solicits a prostitute a felon. They want the prostitute treated as a victim. They have already created a situation that puts the family unit at peril and now they want to do more. I began to see the aliens point. Maybe there is a reason that all human religions place women in a subservient position.

CHAPTER TWENTY

The Greatest Threat to Humanity

These revelations were beginning to open my eyes to events going on all around me and their profound impact on the human species. I asked: "What do you think is the greatest threat to mankind today?"

Their response was, "political correctness."

Everyone has heard of political correctness. When anyone says something in public, the PC police immediately start to dissect the statement so they can identify anything that someone or some group might find offensive. I never realized just how pervasive this phenomenon is until the aliens brought it up.

Not long ago, I told a story about my youth spent in West Palm Beach, Florida. When I was in Junior High, it was common for students to make comments degrading the clothing worn by their peers. The most common and cruelest cut was to say, "Where did you get those clothes, Resale's for Retards?" With the PC Police lurking everywhere, I was quick to point out that there was a huge second hand store named "Resale's for Retards" by the airport in West Palm Beach during the 1960's. The name was on the roof in letters about ten feet tall. You could see them from quite a distance. The store was a precursor to the Goodwill stores that are everywhere today. You could buy shirts for ten cents, shoes for fifteen or twenty cents and even a sport coat for a quarter. My family was very poor back then so most of my clothes were bought there. I knew the store well and feared that the other kids would find out that's where my clothes came from. When I recently told this story, it was met with total disbelief. No one would believe that "Resale's for Retards" was the name of the store. Many people were uncomfortable that I even told the story. Somehow, they felt that I was not being PC by even acknowledging that this ever happened.

This leads to other examples of political correctness and their impact on society. You can no longer say "retard" or "moron." Both of these were perfectly legitimate medical terms at one time. Today you must say "special needs" or just "special."

Remember the recent outcry when a professor used the word "niggardly" to describe someone who was cutting his budget. It is a perfectly descriptive word that you can find in any dictionary. The PC police immediately branded it "racist" and the poor man was close to losing his job. The word describes someone who gives you or your program minimal and reluctant support. It has no racial connotation whatsoever.

How did the word gay become the label for homosexuals? What does being happy have to do with being homosexual? What is this week's acceptable label for African-Americans? When I was young, you were considered upper crust and polite when you referred to them as "Negros." During my life it went from Colored to Negro to Blacks, and now African-Americans. What's next?

As a child, I played cowboys and Indians. Where did my parents go wrong? Obviously, it should have been cowboys and Native Americans.

I know it's not a matter for the PC police but one of my pet peeves is the misuse of the word "utilize." Shallow thinkers believe that saying utilize instead of use, makes them seem smarter. The dictionary tells us that "utilize" is appropriate when you use something in a creative way for something other than its intended purpose. If you use a table to eat dinner on, it is used for its intended purpose. If you stack boxes on top of a table, then use it for a ladder to reach a light bulb, you are utilizing it for something that is not its original intended purpose. You can still say, "Use" but "utilize" is also appropriate.

Getting back to the PC police, imagine my chagrin when I learned that the Atlanta Braves were degrading Native Americans everywhere with their tomahawk chop and the name "Braves." I am now properly ashamed that I used to follow along with the chant and the tomahawk chop as they tried to inspire their players to hit one out of the park or one of their great pitchers to strike out the opposing batter. (Yes, this is sarcasm).

High Schools and colleges all over America have had to change their mascots, team names, and quit playing certain songs because of political correctness. I really do not think there was a studied attempt by school administrators to create such a heinous situation. At some point, they must have thought the mascots, names, and songs were light hearted and evoked a gay spirit. That means happy, not homosexual.

Some changes are generational. When someone says "Thank you," I say, "You are welcome." A lot of people now respond to "Thank you" with "No problem." In what universe is "No problem" a respectful reply to "Thank you?" "No problem" seems to denigrate the value of whatever you were saying "Thank you" for. Is this an attempt at humility? I am not sure of the basis for this new answer but I really believe that there was nothing wrong with the old one. Again, the alien leader and I agree wholeheartedly.

There are so many examples of political correctness causing problems in America. An amazing paradigm shift has resulted in the rights of loud, often obnoxious individuals being more important than the best interest of the species. If you believe in conspiracies, you could make a case that the Democratic Party wants to control America by keeping the majority of the population dependant on government handouts. More than fifty million people are on Medicaid. More than forty million are on welfare. More than ten million receive unemployment insurance payments. Around forty seven per cent of Americans pay no taxes at all yet are the primary recipients of the programs listed above.

Whatever happened to the work ethic in America? My Great Grandfather would not apply for his Social Security benefits until my Grandfather convinced him it was not welfare. He actually paid into the system and earned the Social Security benefit. He was not alone in adamantly opposing any kind of welfare as long as he was able to work. Today there are generations of families that know every trick and boondoggle to receive a government handout.

I believe that when a person cannot work, that person should receive some form of assistance. When you choose not to work or you work "off the books" so you can qualify for government assistance that is un-American. The Constitution never promised cradle to grave government payouts to any and all. In spite of that, there is a constantly growing entitlement mentality today in America.

One of the causes may be the diminished emphasis on competition while children are participating in team activities. Today these activities are designed to develop socialization skills instead of competitive skills. When I was a child, your team got a trophy if you won more games than the other teams. Sometime in the recent past, it was determined by people with too much time on their hands that this made the losers feel bad about themselves. They believe that every child should be given a trophy just for participation. This would make every child feel good just for showing up and build their self esteem. The theory sounds good but the long term feelings of entitlement that it engenders trump the temporary joy of receiving a trophy. You must learn that you have to earn rewards. They are not going to be given to you just for showing up.

There are so many people in the workforce today that think that if they simply show up for work every day, they deserve promotions, bonuses, and other considerations. When a person who really works hard enters the mix, they don't know how to act. Usually they just hate the hard worker and do everything they can to pull them down. How dare they work hard and make everyone else look bad!

Social promotions in schools came along so you wouldn't feel bad about being left behind. Some parents went overboard and demanded that their children be treated special (not retarded) no matter what they did. Parents would not allow their children to be disciplined at school. Lawsuits were filed with the result that teachers could no longer control their classrooms. How could this be bad? What are the longer term effects of the improved feelings of self esteem created in this manner? The sense of entitlement this engenders carries on throughout life.

People began to feel and truly believe that they are owed consideration for just being here. Why don't I make as much as the guy who risked everything to establish a viable business? Just because I didn't go to college, I shouldn't be paid less than the ones who did. I could go on. An example of this entitlement mentality should suffice. There was a young man with some talent whose father was in a position of influence on a police force. Every time the young man got into a jam, his father fixed it for him. Speeding tickets, driving his motorcycle on the golf course, even petty theft were all covered by his father's position. The young man grew up and his father retired from the police force. The man got a speeding ticket and was outraged! He had been a speeder all his life. Imagine the audacity of a policeman to give him a ticket! He was serving in the Army and thought it was a good idea to steal a carburetor from a car belonging to one of his roommates. He was kicked out of the Army. Again, he just couldn't understand it.

He drifted from one job to another where he convinced himself that he was always "done wrong" by his boss. He got unemployment when possible, food stamps, and any other government assistance he could. He would work for cash so it did not interfere with his government check. One of his children was handicapped so he and his ex-wife would fight over custody of this child, because the child came with a government check. Custody of their other child was not so important since he was seen as a liability and not an asset.

Years passed and his whole life was based on "getting by." There was never any hint of striving for a better life for your children or setting an example to emulate so his offspring would try to break out of this welfare mentality. To establish that this man actually had a modicum of talent, he worked out every angle that would allow him to get by. He could tell you how many days late you could pay your light bill before the power company would turn the power off. He also knew how to turn the meter back on and how long it would take the power company to actually pull the meter when you don't pay. He knew how to get his utilities turned on in his name, his wife's name, his children's name. He developed this knowledge for the purpose of being able to get by when his power was turned off. It was never a question of if it was turned off. It was just a question of when it would be turned off.

This same thinking applied to everything he ever did. If he rented a house, he knew how many months he could stay there without paying the rent. If he bought a car, and didn't make his payments, he knew how long he could hide it before it was repossessed. If someone in his family had a fever, he didn't go to the drug store for aspirin. He took them to the emergency room at the local hospital. He had no insurance but knew that the emergency room could not turn him away. He was not stupid. He was programmed from youth to be dependent on the system. His attitude and lifestyle is pervasive all over America today. A lot of the people I know, that are about his age and from his social level live by similar rules. There are generations of this type of behavior being exhibited and no end in sight. No wonder the aliens think we are a lost cause. I admit that I have thought so myself.

116

The last example represents the lower end of the social scale. The other end of the social scale can be just as dangerous. This is the group that the PC police come from. When did the hyphen become a symbol of separation from the norm? Why do some women think it necessary to put a hyphen in their name so they retain their old name as they add a married name? The hyphen seems to bring baggage with it. It's like they have something to prove since they've drawn attention to themselves with a hyphen.

There is a lady traveling around the United States who inspects the playgrounds at fast food restaurants. She is not paid to do this. She is allegedly on vacation but she is inspecting her way across the country. She says she is concerned about the cleanliness of these playgrounds and wants to bring national attention to this mess. I understand her concern for the playgrounds her children use and she has the right to support only businesses with clean playgrounds. I have to ask, who made her the Crusader for playground cleanliness? Does she hope to create a job for herself as playground inspector by embarrassing companies who do not adhere to her standards of cleanliness? We know she likes attention since she uses the hyphen in her name. Is this just an attempt to gain attention on a broader scale? Maybe that's it. The jury is still out on this one.

It was probably someone with a hyphen in her name that caused the national uproar over bicycle safety. Millions of children have ridden bicycles for years without helmets, shoulder pads, and knee pads. More importantly, they lived to tell about it. Sure, we all suffered our share of scrapes and torn off toenails. I don't recall ever knowing a child that died from simply falling off a bicycle. There probably have been some somewhere, but have children suddenly become so fragile that they must be totally insulated from the world as they ride their bikes?

According to statistics, more people are killed while on bicycles since they started to share the road with automobiles. When we were kids, we gave cars the right of way. Now bicyclists think that since they are "green" they should have equal access to travel on the roads.

Back when children used their imaginations instead of using computer games to create an altered universe, the bike could become a horse as you played cowboys and Indians (Native Americans). We clipped a playing card on the frame so it could bounce off the spokes, making a noise that turned it into a motorcycle. Sometimes my bike was a jet fighter or a rocket to space. We rode in the summer so we could feel the cool breeze rustling through our hair.

How can you spontaneously do these things when you must begin by suiting up like you are going into battle? Maybe this is all a government trick to get children used to wearing battle armor so when they are fighting the next big threat to American values, they can be ready. This makes as much sense as any other hypothesis.

Look at the Boy Scouts. Most people don't realize that Lord Baden Powell created the Boy Scouts in England because city dwellers didn't make good soldiers. He created the Boy Scouts to teach kids basic camp skills, not to mention the love of uniforms and decorations, so that they would be better soldiers as adults. The Hitler Youth was slammed for doing much the same thing but they got a lot of bad press because their side lost the war.

People like this, with so much time on their hands, are why barber shops are now hair salons. Getting a haircut at the barber shop was a simple thing. You came in and sat down. While you waited for the next available barber, you read some old magazines or the barber told you dirty stories. The haircut didn't cost much and there were no women in sight.

The hair salon is a different matter. Most of them require an appointment. There are women everywhere cutting, dyeing, shampooing, and talking about how bad men are in general. There are no dirty stories being told and the haircuts are very expensive. One thing I've noticed is that the talk among the women in the salon seems to focus on the most dire projections for the future. They talk about how too little rain will cause food prices to go up. They talk about how too much rain will cause food prices to go up. They talk about heinous crimes and how laws should be tougher and how bad things are getting. I've never heard them talk about how wonderful it is to be alive. I guess happiness is out of style.

This reminds me of the time down in Alabama when a bunch of people gossiping at a hair salon created a gas shortage in three counties. Someone went to the hair salon and told that her friend was a truck driver who delivered fuel to area gas stations. He told her that this was the last delivery he was going to make for awhile. He said no more or no less than that. She embellished his statement by telling everyone who would listen that there would be no more gas after this delivery. The cell phones came alive with the news. "You better fill up your car and buy all the gas you can because there was going to be a shortage for at least a month." There were lines at all the gas stations. Fist fights broke out as people tried to break line or took too long buying their gas. Some stations raised the price a dollar a gallon on the spot. Within hours, there was no gas available for sale in three counties. Later, it came out that the truck driver was going on vacation and wasn't going to be back for a month. Someone else was scheduled to make deliveries while he was gone. There was no gas shortage except the artificial one created by sensationalism and exaggeration.

Elroy suggested that we take a little trip so I could see a planet where the experiment actually seemed to be working out. He said they have seeded many planets throughout the universe and they are all progressing at different levels. I thought this would be great so away we went.

We went back to the bridge and Elroy adjusted the controls for our trip. There was that weird feeling and then the stars all changed. One moment the star patterns we see every day from earth and the next, it was all different. Elroy told me that we were many light years from Earth. It certainly looked like nothing I had ever seen before except for the bluish green planet just ahead. It seemed to have a little more surface water than Earth. The continents looked a lot smaller and were scattered across the ocean like a string of islands on Earth. Elroy told me that the life forms here developed from dolphin-like creatures. They rested in the water but came onto the land to work. My alien enhanced brain had no problem grasping this concept even though it was so different from Earth. The creatures of this planet had no war, no weapons of mass destruction, no pollution problems, and generally lived in peace and harmony with one another and the planet.

"How is this possible?" I asked.

Elroy replied: "They have one leader, one government, one race, and plenty for everyone to eat. The leader is the smartest dolphin on the planet. If a smarter one is born, it becomes

120

leader once it is fully mature. There is no conflict over it. The system conforms to the laws of nature where the best individual rises to the top. They all accept it and support the system."

Although it seems to smack of the Chinese communist ethos that "we should be happy in our work" their system does seem to be successful. At least it does on a planet owned and operated by dolphins. I'm not so sure if it can work so well on a planet like ours with many races, plenty of war, weapons of mass destruction everywhere, pollution, and rapidly depleting natural resources. Somewhere we must have taken a wrong turn or turns.

This trip gave me a real yard stick to measure where we humans stand on the evolutionary scale. I'm afraid that we are not nearly as advanced as we like to think we are.

Although we traveled many light years there and back, the whole trip seemed to take no time. Once we got back into Earth orbit, the alien observations continued.

CHAPTER TWENTY ONE

Fear Sells

People seem to love fear. The news on television always takes the most pessimistic position possible. When a person is arrested for a crime, they immediately report that person may face thirty years to life in prison or some other stiff sentence, with "if convicted" often omitted entirely. When the weather is stormy, they break into the regularly scheduled program so you can be scared into watching them. They drone on endlessly about what could, possibly, maybe, might happen if conditions develop in just the right way. It's their moment in the sun. It's their time to shine but it all falls apart if you are not scared.

Recently there were horrible tornados across the South. Many people were killed and a lot of property was damaged. I blame some of the deaths on the "Chicken Little the sky is falling" reporting of television news. When every cloud in the sky is reported as a possible tornado from which you must seek shelter immediately, you become somewhat immune to the fear and deaf to the warnings. I believe that many people thought this was just more of the same sensationalistic reporting and ignored the warnings. How can you be expected to know the difference between sensationalism and fact?

Have you ever noticed the attraction that auto accidents have for people? An accident on the other side of an interstate highway can cause traffic jams for miles as people slow down to see what happened. I've personally witnessed people parking more than half mile away so they can walk to a wreck and see the extent of the damage. If you are the first on the scene and you might be of help, I understand and totally agree that it's your civic duty to stop. When an accident site is obviously under control, it is truly ghoulish behavior to want to see the wreck just because you are nosey and you might see somebody maimed or dead. To me that's pretty creepy behavior if that's actually the reason you stopped.

Years ago, I had a neighborhood video shop. Everybody wanted to see the latest movies but sometimes they were all rented out. The number one, all time biggest money maker in the whole store, filled with over ten thousand titles, was a series of low budget videos called "The Faces of Death." These were actual shots of people being killed around the world that had been captured as news footage. The fact that these were not staged but were absolutely real captivated the audience. Some families rented them over and over. I guess they enjoyed them so much, they wanted to share the experience with their friends. They were so thoughtful!

CHAPTER TWENTY TWO

Back to the Aliens

The discussion with the aliens was proceeding seemingly at the speed of light. The more we communicated telepathically, the easier it got. We traded thoughts at such speed it was hard to tell if it was my thoughts or theirs. I could see the events they described as if I was actually there. Although the exchange of information was amazing and the most interesting situation I ever found myself in, even my alien enhanced body could not keep up. Gradually, I became so tired that I once again slipped into a restless sleep, right there on that comfortable chair.

When I woke up, I tried to pretend that I was still asleep. I laid there for a long time with thoughts of all the things we discussed racing through my head. There were so many things that happened throughout history that I had never even heard of. The aliens described these events in such a matter of fact manner that I couldn't help believing they were true. Sometimes I peeked at the aliens from narrowly opened eyes, mainly because I still wasn't sure if the whole thing was real or some kind of fantastic dream. It wasn't a dream.

One thing I forgot is that the aliens are telepathic. When I started thinking about whether they were real or not, they all erupted into a high pitched warbling that I learned was laughter. Since they knew I was awake, I jumped up and hurried into the alien "bathroom". I was really starting to enjoy their version of a shower. If I could just take this invention home with me, I'd really have something!

When I came out, there was more food lined up on a table behind the chair I was sitting in. Other than no meat, there was a nice variety of tasty entrees for me to choose from. Putting some things on a plate, I sat down and the discussion started again.

CHAPTER TWENTY THREE

We Become the Borg

The aliens mentioned human's connection to computer games and how that has diminished the imaginary play of children. The aliens were concerned about what this would lead to. Nature abhors a vacuum. Once the internet was created, it began to be filled with information. Some of it is useful, while a lot of it just serves as a waste of time. Once the aliens brought up the subject, I took over the lecture. My alien mental enhancement allowed me to put together some random events that I never before realized were connected. Here are my observations on the rampaging effects of technology.

The growth of social networks caused a regression to the primal herding instincts of humans. As the opportunities to stay connected to the herd grow, you see more and more people falling prey to this type of technology. People try to text and drive and constantly check their portable communication devices (they are more than just a telephone) instead of taking part in live, human to human conversation. Two people sitting at a table in a restaurant, each on their individual cell phones talking to someone else and not to each other is a common sight. The same situation takes place in cars.

I've been in a group of twenty people and eighteen of them were doing something with a communications device that kept them out of the immediate conversation. Cell phones, the iPad, laptops, secret agent spy scopes and who knows what else are being used to stay constantly in touch with other members of the herd. People can't drive without talking on cell phones. All day at work there is a constant flow of people into the hallways and out of doors to connect with mysterious persons on the other end. They all have traditional phones on their desks but the lure of the exotic has them standing outside in temperatures ranging from near zero to around 100 degrees to make that cell phone connection. Rain and snow don't stop them either!

Not that long ago I spent some time in Hawaii where I was supervising production of a television commercial for the Navy. A few people in America know that a few years ago they changed their "brand" from "Accelerate Your Life" to "America's Navy: A Global Force for Good." These commercials are designed to teach the rest of America about the change.

After several years of "accelerating your life" a few non-Navy personnel were finally recognizing the phrase as representing the Navy. Just when it was catching on, the Navy decided to change it. I could go into the reasons why this occurred but you would feel sure I was lying if I told you. Most people didn't realize that the Navy had a "brand." They knew about the ships and planes and stuff but really couldn't see how the Navy needed a brand.

They aren't selling anything except the opportunity to have a job when you get right down to it. Every other selling point is just icing on the cake. Anyway, just as they changed course, the bottom fell out of the economy and people began to beat down the Navy's doors trying to get a job. The Navy is suddenly so popular that people often wait around a year just to get in. With recruiting going so well there was no need to spend a lot of money on advertising so Big Navy cut the advertising budget. Did you ever try to launch a new brand or slogan with no money? It's not a pretty sight. The reduced advertising budget means there is very little money to buy TV time to play our commercials but the production of new commercials is funded by another account. That's why we still make new ones even though we don't get to play the ones we already have often enough for anyone to remember them.

Let's get back to the point. When I observe the demonstrated need to stay connected by electronic devices, it never fails to amaze me. On the airplane going to Hawaii, I observed a young couple on their honeymoon. They sat next to each other with each deeply absorbed by their personal portable communications device. They didn't look longingly at each other with that newlywed hunger in their eyes. Their full concentration was focused on their cell phone. Now I know that even calling their portable communication device a "cell phone" makes me a dinosaur but whatever attributes they have now, they started as a telephone. One of the techno geeks explained to me that they are really tiny portable computers that also have a telephone function. The main function I see is that they keep people from face to face communications. What could be so important on that tiny device that would keep newlyweds absolutely spellbound?

During that trip I also had the opportunity to fly by chartered aircraft to the island of Molocai. It is famous for being a leper colony where they used to throw the lepers out of a boat near the cliffs. If the leper survived to make it to the island, then they had a new home. Despite its rather sordid history, Molocai is still beautiful with the cliffs rising straight up out of the ocean. There is very little beach there. Most of what I saw was rocky shoreline. It is a sight that most people will never get a chance to see.

There was also no cell phone signal where we landed on Molocai. Early on I noticed the other members of my group going through withdrawals as they were cut off from the collective. After several hours on the island, you can imagine their distress. When we finally flew back to Honolulu, everyone but me was locked head down on their cell phones. They occasionally grunted a comment to one another without raising their heads as if every moment connected to the internet was precious. For me the choice was simple. Do I enjoy a magnificent once in a lifetime view or focus all my attention on the object in my hand? Is this evolution or devolution?

A TV commercial I saw the other night sums it all up nicely. A younger female was sitting alone in front of her computer. She was complaining that her parents were so backwards and technologically challenged. She had finally convinced them to start a Facebook page but they only had about fifteen friends. They were too busy playing golf and tennis and outside doing things with other people. She had over six hundred friends on Facebook so she felt was really living. Of course with all those Facebook friends to keep up with, she never had time to actually do anything. For me there is an obvious message here but will the younger female and those like her ever get it?

Other extremes exist in the pimply faced, Surge Cola drinking, can't get a date to the prom, computer geeks and nerds who live in their mother's basement and stay connected to chat rooms, game sites, social sites, and blogs night and day. They always have something to say and it seems that now they finally have a platform that makes them feel important and that people will listen to. You read their comments on how good the things they like are, but more often how bad everything else is. They routinely expound about the merits of movies and books but mostly the lack of merit of same, when they have never produced a thing. They are self proclaimed experts who have their minute in the sun while never leaving the basement. Obviously this hit a nerve with me.

One of my pet peeves is critics who have never produced a thing having the audacity to castigate a film or book based on their self proclaimed insight. A friend of mine has directed more than two hundred movies. They are seen all over the world on premium TV channels and are available at your video outlet of choice. He would not have been able to direct so many pictures if he wasn't good at what he does. If you read the comments offered up by many of these geeks and nerds you would think he is a no talent hack. After reading some of their comments, I am convinced that many times they never saw the movie or read the book they are talking about.

Surely this is harmless, right? Let's look at where we were, where we are now, and where we are headed. A few years ago we spent time outside, enjoying nature as we drove, biked, walked, or flew. Cell phones yet to be invented. When we went outside, we could disconnect from the cares of the world because we were out of reach. Car phones were invented. Bag phones closely followed. Phones got smaller and smaller. Some smart guy decided that it would be cool to copy the "communicator" from early Star Trek episodes so they created the "flip phone." Maybe that is what put the portable communications device over the hump. It went from a novelty item to a must have. More and more people got them. They evolved from simple telephones to multi-media devices.

In a parallel development, computers went from the size of buildings to desk top devices. Soon laptop computers appeared on the market. Everyone who was someone had a cell phone, a laptop, a pad or tablet, and probably a desk top computer at home or the office or in both places. Some smart guy created social networks and designed games to play, alternate universes people could pretend to live in, multiple reasons why people had to stay connected at all times. They started combining computers and telephones so that your phone can do a little of everything now.

People have a zombie-like attachment to their electronic gadgets. During business meetings, I see people surreptitiously peeking at their gadgets every few seconds as if something earth shaking might occur and they would be left out through inattention.

Recently, I was sitting in a class filled with Navy Chiefs, waiting to lecture them on what the Navy Advertising Plans Division does to support the Navy's recruiting. There was a Navy Lieutenant also waiting to lecture. I noticed that he seemed to be fascinated by his cell phone. A closer look revealed that he was playing a game on the cell phone while the other Department Heads gave their presentations. I estimated his age to be in the early thirties.

I mention his age only to show that games on telephones are not just for kids anymore. The same is true of on-line games. Several members of the staff are hooked on on-line gaming. They spend every available second playing and ascending to ever higher levels of difficulty. The demonstrated commitment required to spend time this way simply evades me.

In a few years, people probably won't leave their homes. They will all be "pimply faced, Surge Cola drinking, can't get a date to the prom, computer geeks and nerds who live in their mother's basement and stay connected to chat rooms, game sites, social sites, and blogs night and day." They will surface intermittently to do the minimum work required to keep them alive, and then dive back into the security of the electronic universe. It is easy to imagine a time when losing connectivity will create a traumatic experience that reduces the subject to a quivering mass.

Computer dependence is already leading to de-evolution of the herd. Whole generations have lost the ability to perform simple math problems like making change in a commercial transaction.

Just the other day, while having lunch, one of my associates witnessed a startling tableau. While attempting to pay for his super-sized, fast food meal, he discovered that the young lady behind the counter was new on the job. He became aware of this when she had to ask the manager to enter the transaction into the point of sale computer. The manager entered the transaction and walked away. The total cost of the meal was six dollars even. He gave the clerk a ten dollar bill. She stood there with a blank look on her face. She didn't know how much change to give back. As she explained, when keying in a transaction, you were supposed to type in how much the customer gave you. The computer would then tell you how much change to give back. Since the manager simply keyed in the transaction without entering the amount the customer gave her, she could not possibly know what to give back. She stood there until the manager came back to see why the line was backing up. The manager was about two generations removed from the clerk and was still functionally literate. He said with an exasperated tone of voice, "Give the man four dollars."

Another acquaintance has a wife who is a school teacher. Her students are from generally middle income families. Every one of them has the latest communications device and wears trendy clothing. She announced a pop quiz the other day and more than half the class didn't have simple class materials like pen and paper with them. Others complained that a pop test would be unfair because some didn't have their iPhones with them. They had no way to look up the answers. Her other complaint concerns the negative impact on spelling that texting has wrought.

Have you ever tried to read and understand a text message when your generation began life with no telephone at all? Back then people had ink pins with replaceable nibs and leaky ink cartridges. For many of us generationally challenged folks, we just don't understand why you would want to type on your telephone anyway? It's first and foremost a telephone. You can actually talk to the person on the other end!

In this day of huge flat screen televisions, why would you want to download and watch a movie on a tiny screen on the face of your telephone? If I went to the trouble of downloading a movie, I would want to be able to see it. Most movie downloads aren't free. I just don't get it.

The nerd herd also loves the new downloadable books. Soon, there will be people who have never realized the joy of turning the pages in a regular old book. They don't realize the contribution to the wisdom of mankind that we owe to the book. Before the printing press people were pretty much in the dark. Up to that time, books were hand written. Some of them took up to a year to write out, in ink, by hand.

The church made sure that only religious books were made available since they were the main ones doing the printing. After the printing press, books were finally available to the common man. More books meant more knowledge spread around. There was less dependence on the church for information. They really hate that. Information is power. Control the information and you control the people.

Libraries sprang up to contain and share the knowledge contained in books. Do you remember the old days when devoted parents would purchase a set of encyclopedia for their home? If you had little money, you could actually buy them over a period of time. I've seen poor mothers purchase an entire set encyclopedia, one volume at a time. They wanted their children to have access to an educational asset that they didn't have growing up. When was the last time you saw a door-to-door encyclopedia salesman or even saw a commercial for a complete set of encyclopedia on television? Google and Wikipedia pretty much made them obsolete.

With the advent of the "electronic book" ownership of books could become obsolete. There is a commercial that shows a vast pile of books while another person stands there with some sort of electronic book replacement. The electronic book is said to contain the whole pile of books displayed there. They view that as a great thing. They value the convenience and the savings in space by storing all the books on one device. They do not realize that they can now misplace or damage one item and lose all the information contained in one stroke. If I lost one thousand books, I would be devastated. Book downloads are not exactly cheap either. If you shop around, you can get real books for very little money and it is yours forever. You can read it as many times as you like and even share it with your friends. Will you lend your electronic book to a friend to read one of the thousand books stored on it?

As a child, I remember riding my bicycle over the half mile of dirt and gravel road to the nearest paved road, so that I could meet the bookmobile. It was a small library on wheels that delivered books to rural areas during the summer months when kids didn't have access to the school library. You could request books and they would bring them during their every other week deliveries. I always checked out all the books they would allow me to. The limit was ten books and I always checked out the full number allowed. Safely riding in the basket on the handlebars of my second hand bike, I took my books and rode home as quickly as possible. I would prioritize the books, always saving the best for last. I'd stack them in order by my bed, grab the first one in line and head for my favorite reading place. I'd pull up a jumbo sweet onion from the garden, and then I'd climb on top of the well house so I could reach the lower branches of a medium sized pecan tree. I'd swing up into the pecan tree and nestle among the branches, munch on my fresh sweet onion, and read the first book cover to cover. We didn't have air conditioning so the feel of the breeze and the cool shade offered by the pecan tree were a wonderful setting for taking an imaginary journey through reading a real book.

What will happen one day when all the libraries are gone because the nerd herd wants everything fed to them on their personal communication device? How about audio books and their effect on literacy? I know people who will listen to books while driving but won't read a book on a bet. Magazines and newspapers are also feeling the pressure to go out of print and just go on line. Book stores are closing at an alarming rate. When they are all gone, books will become an oddity. Imagine what will happen in the future when books are gone and every piece of information comes to you directly from the central collective. That sounds like the Borg from Star Trek, doesn't it? Remember what happens to the Borg when cut off from the collective? They go mad because they can't stand the feeling of being alone. Will the dependence on social networks and the drive to stay connected lead us to a "Borg-like" existence?

What if something should occur that terminates all technology and eliminates electronic transfer of information such as a monster solar flare? All electronic books, all web based interaction, most of man's stored knowledge could vanish in an instant. With books and other printed material gone away as obsolete and backwards, the step from superior to savage could occur in one step. Technology is great but there is always a price to pay if you don't understand the lessons of the past. The greatest library in the history of mankind existed in Alexandria, Egypt. The greatest minds of the known world came there to study and add their knowledge to the vast collection of wisdom stored there. When it was burned to the ground, much of mankind's history was burned with it. The loss of the library at Alexandria is the closest thing to the disaster facing us if we become too dependent on gadgets to store our knowledge.

During our last break the aliens took me to see the dolphin world where everybody got along and the alien experiment seemed to be working. Earlier, they showed me the results of the failed experiment on Mars and the total devastation that caused. I asked Elroy if there were other planets that were in the same boat as Earth. Do most of the experiments work out as planned or do more of them fail and have to start over? Elroy pointed out that there are thousands of planets in the universe where life has been seeded. Many of them flourish but an alarming number of them require constant attention. Earth is one of them. They have started the experiment over a couple of times and made many local adjustments hoping to get us on the right path. This time they are taking a hard look at whether it's worth another do-over or if they should just end the project and move on. I don't know about you but I'm in favor of more local adjustments and save the total do-over for another time!

CHAPTER TWENTY FOUR

Why Do Both the Democrats and Republicans Hate America?

The aliens decided that it was time to get to a discussion of politics. They had tap danced around the history of the church and their involvement with the world's government. Now they had some hard questions that they were looking to answer. They had such high hopes for the whole "America" experiment. America has made do with two basic political parties since the beginning.

"Why do both the Republicans and Democrats hate America?" they asked.

You can bet that I was flabbergasted at such a question. "Why do you think that?" I said. They then started reeling it out to me and suddenly it all made sense.

Early in America's history, it seemed that a band of idealists came together and created the dream of America. This was to be a country based on separation of church and state. This was to be a country where the best and brightest could flourish. Competition was encouraged as a way to achieve greatness. Both the political parties loved the idea of America and wanted it to succeed. Sure, they had differences of opinion about how to achieve that success but they never lost sight of the ultimate goal. That goal was to make America the greatest country in the world.

Today, we have two parties that don't seem to care about the American dream. They only want everything their way. Year after year they threaten a government shut down until the other party caves in before passing a budget of some sort. Sometimes it is years before they pass an actual budget. They just pass continuing resolutions allowing them to keep the government open and spending on their pet projects.

When you read about building nuclear submarines in two different ship yards because of pork barrel politics, you sort of understand the reasoning. When you discover that they build one end of the submarine in one ship yard and the other end in another shipyard, and then try to fit the two pieces together, it gets more than a little strange. This is based purely on politics. There is no legitimate reason for doing something so asinine.

Look at the saga of the Littoral Combat Ship. There are two competing designs from shipyards in two separate Congressional districts. One is a radically designed tri-hull and the other is a more traditional style of construction. The tri-hull costs more but out performs the more traditional design. The government paid to have one constructed at each shipyard. Rather than make a decision based on logical factors such as initial cost, performance objectives, range of operations, and so on, they just decided to buy even numbers of both the ships. That way, both Congressional districts got some construction jobs and it didn't make one side or the other feel like a loser.

Do you remember the participation trophies and the sense of entitlement described earlier? That probably comes into play in this decision. Of course both of the current Littoral Combat Ships have tremendous design flaws. Along with many other problems, no one thought that the combination of steel,

139

aluminum, and salt water would create extensive corrosion kind of like on a car battery terminal. They are buying them anyway.

The legendary Bradley Fighting Vehicle was a money drain that went on for twenty years or more. That project cost billions of dollars and produced a pitiful end product. Every new military leader placed in charge of the project would change the specifications. This fit the logic of the modern military mind. If you are in charge, you must place your stamp on anything under you. Changes must be made, whether they are needed or not. Whatever happened to the old saying: "If it ain't broke, don't fix it?" Which of course means, if it works already, why change it?

The F-35 program is another military project that should result in jail time for many of those in charge but will likely end up with medals, promotions, and cash bonuses all around. It is years behind schedule, generated billions of dollars in cost overruns, and has yet to yield an aircraft that meets the standard of simple, safe and cost effective.

It was that kind of thinking that almost crushed American automakers. For years, it was the practice of American automakers to design a car, rush it into production, sell it to unsuspecting consumers and then try to fix the bugs in the design at the dealership where it was sold. Getting a product to market and selling it was the number one ambition. Creating quality products was a distant second. Just sell it, and then fix it later. The rest of the world listened to Dr. Deming who preached that quality should be the number one goal and all repairs should be made before sale to the consumer. He was probably adjusted by the aliens since this was such a radical shift in industrial thinking. No matter where he got the idea, it works. The quality of most foreign cars was perceived to be superior to American cars. This eroded America's position as the world leader in the auto industry.

These days it's hard to find a real American car. Sure, the old names are there like Ford, Chevrolet, and Chrysler but they have parts manufactured in plants all over the world. Chrysler is majority owned by the Italian company Fiat. Even foreign named cars are built in America. Toyota, Kia, Nissan, Mercedes and others have plants in America building cars but does that make them American cars? It's a lot to wrap your head around.

The world economy is so inter-related today that if one country stumbles, the repercussions are felt around the world. With all these considerations in mind, the Republicans and Democrats still play chicken with our economy. For years they have borrowed money to pay the country's bills. They have now hocked our future to the point that they must constantly raise the country's debt limit so they can pay their bills. With a definite date in sight where they will be unable to meet the country's obligations, they have a great deal of trouble agreeing on a compromise which will enable them to raise the debt limit. If it was you or me, we would just cut back on spending until we could live within our means but that's for us small fish. The sharks that run our government don't care about the future. They simply want everything now. If you listen to the rhetoric going on you see that neither side wants to cut any real spending. Any time they do offer to cut spending, the fine print shows that the cuts will begin years in the future. Long after the current occupants of the congressional seats and the oval office have moved on to greener pastures.

Going back to the conspiracy theory, the Democrats seem to want to keep all their social programs going because that's how they get votes. The Republicans want to only cut social programs because that hurts the Democrats. The billions of dollars we send to countries that hate us are never mentioned as places to cut. Fighting wars in places that don't want us there and trying to rebuild the economies of third world countries while our economic infrastructure falls apart is ludicrous.

A lot of our leaders seem to think that the rest of the world wants to be just like us. That is not really true. They would like to have our wealth but do not want to adopt our government and social values. They have their own. People everywhere just want a piece of the pie. They want a safe neighborhood, food on the table, and the chance at a happy life. Offering foreigners a hand out if they become copies of us is just wrong. Our system of government will not work everywhere. Many countries require a stronger central government than we Americans would tolerate. Guess what? Most of the people of the world don't care what form of government they have as long as it provides a safe neighborhood, food on the table, and the chance at a happy life. As long as they know what the rules are, they will be happy. It's when you go changing the rules that the trouble starts. That is what we have tried to do over and over. Yet we still act surprised when it doesn't work out like we thought it would. Einstein said that the definition of insanity is doing the same thing over and over again and expecting different results.

The economy of the United States faced a meltdown in August of 2011 without immediate action being taken on the debt ceiling. They still held out. One of the Republican offers would be a temporary fix that would cause the problem to reappear during the 2012 elections. The Democrats temporary fix would postpone any additional debt ceiling problems until after the 2012 elections. Could this be any more transparent? Neither party had the good of the country at heart. They both only consider the impact on their own chances for re-election and control of the presidency.

While they did finally come to an agreement to increase the debt ceiling, the deal was not strong enough to do anything about balancing the budget or significantly reducing the government's debt. Neither side wanted to give up anything. The credit rating of the United States was lowered and the world stock market took a nose dive after their compromise.

The alien leader expressed total amazement at this attitude. Not only are they amazed that both parties have evolved into such self serving entities, they wonder why the populace keeps voting them into office. That is the real dilemma. Ask almost anyone on the street and they will voice their disgust with the games the political parties are playing. When voting time comes, they place their votes for the incumbent and rarely make changes. Basically, once elected, the office is yours for as long as you want it. Only term limits, death, or being caught with your britches down will get you out of office.

It is rare once you have a taste of power that you willingly give it up. This is an example of the herd mentality prevalent among humans. Voters typically vote for the incumbent. In one county, the Sheriff was elected to office and served for about 35 years. His son, who had the same name as the father, was then elected and served for 25 years. For many years most people thought they were still voting for the father. The son was finally cast out of office when he tried to retire for a day so he could collect his state pension. He then planned to be re-elected to office and collect his full pay plus his retirement check. Once this was revealed, he was voted out. He was "caught with his britches down."

CHAPTER TWENTY FIVE

Religion and the Law

The mixture of religion and government has always been repugnant to the true American. Today you hear politicians who pander to the extreme right spout idiocies like "we need more Jesus in our country!" "We need more Bible in our laws!" They say that a return to Biblical Judgment would make us more successful because then God would bless us. Plenty of them believe that God is punishing America for embracing the gay lifestyle, legalizing abortions, and a general propensity for living un-Godly lives.

Have any of them ever lived in a theocracy? Have they experienced first-hand what happens in a nation where the religious police have the upper hand and supersede the law of man? I have seen it first hand and it is not a pretty sight. No American would tolerate such a system yet without really thinking about it, they seem to endorse a return to the Old Testament. Most, but not all, Moslem countries use the Koran as the law of the land. In Turkey, they have a separation with secular law taking precedence over holy law. Mustafa Kemal Atatürk was the first president of modern Turkey. He established a program of political, economic, and cultural reforms to transform the former Ottoman Empire into a modern, westernized, and secular nation-state. Turkey is a

Muslim nation in terms of religion. It is a secular nation in terms of government. In Saudi Arabia, the Cradle of Islam, the Koran is the law. Religious police, called the Mutawa'ah, are free to arrest you for any violation of the rules outlined in the Koran. If they say you are guilty, then you are guilty. There is no court of appeals, no trial by your peers and so on, like in America. There are no rules of evidence or legal technicalities that can get you off. If they arrest you, they dictate the penalty, and you are punished. Punishment may include prison, cutting off a hand, cutting off your head, or even stoning. There are no appeals. What happens if the Mutawa'ah, a body of humans with the power to enforce religious law, simply does not like you? What about when they are having a bad day and feel especially put out by your otherwise innocuous behavior? You pay the price and there is nothing anyone can do about it.

It kind of takes you back to the old days of the Salem Witch trials. Anyone could accuse you of witchcraft. The authorities (good Christians one and all) would hold your head under water to establish whether you were a witch. If you died, you were not a witch. If you didn't drown, you were guilty of witchcraft and you were killed. Sounds like a foolproof solution.

It is believed that Mutawa'ah are charged with this responsibility by Allah and would never allow human frailties to interfere with God's judgment. What-ever happened to the saying: "Power corrupts and absolute power corrupts absolutely?" There was a documentary on Islamic law as applied in Afghanistan on HBO one night. They followed some people who had been imprisoned for violations of the Koran. A man and a young woman were arrested for having premarital sex. The girl was pregnant. He and his family claimed that she climbed in the window of their home and had sex with the young man in his bed. The woman and her family claimed that he came into her room and raped her. After about three months in prison, an arrangement was made by the families for the two prisoners to marry each other. They appeared before a judge and were married.

Part of the marriage process was the negotiation of the bride price and dowry. Another key issue was the amount of money the bride should receive if they divorced. With these issues cleared up, the marriage was confirmed. The judge then determined that according to Islamic law, the family was the most important thing. Since they married each other, then the crime became less serious. He gave them each four months in prison and they left together, three days later.

In another case, a young woman and young man were arrested while eating dinner together in his parent's house. Nothing was going on other than eating together. They were both taken to prison. After months during which she was given a very through physical examination, it was discovered that she was still technically a virgin. However, it appeared that she may have had anal sex. After exhaustive questioning, the girl admitted that they had anal intercourse several times so that she could still be a virgin. She wanted him to marry her and claimed that he said he loved her and wanted to marry her. Once they had sex, he changed his mind. Her parents tried to arrange a marriage between the two but it was not to be. The judge asked if they would marry, and the answer was no. She was given a three year sentence. I'm not sure what sentence the man received but it was less than the woman.

Another case involved a woman who was arrested for running away from home. She was a divorced woman who felt restricted by her family at home. She ran away and hid at the home of a woman who wanted her to marry her son. She begged and pleaded with the girl to marry her son but she would not do so. Even when faced with a long prison sentence, she would not marry the son. This case was even stranger because they arrested the lady who sheltered the runaway. She was in prison too. She felt that if she could get the woman to marry her son, the charge would go away and she would be released. The woman would have been a second wife for the son and the mother thought she would be good for the family. No deal was made so the judge sentenced the girl to 18 months for running away from home and the woman who sheltered her to 12 months in prison. The runaway mentioned that she was afraid that her family would quietly kill her once she got out since she had brought such shame to the family.

The Koran, Old Testament, and the Torah are all based on the same early religious writings. They are essentially the same with just a few minor differences. Is this really the way we want our laws to work. Remember, stoning is still a valid punishment in the Old Testament. The death penalty by stoning applies to pre-marital sex and being rude to your parents. I don't think this would be a big hit in America. That is, unless we used it as a population control device.

You see the same attitudes in American police without the added incentive of believing that they are anointed by God to perform this task. Studies show, as well as casual observation, that most police feel that they can do anything at all and it's OK. They feel that they are above the rules because they enforce the rules. How many times do you see the police doing a u-turn in the middle of the road for no apparent reason? Why do they think they should be allowed to drive as fast as they want to, even as they give the rest of us speeding tickets for doing the same thing? How often do you see them rolling through a stop sign? How often do you see them with an arrogant and hostile attitude as they write you up for an infraction that they are regularly guilty of? You have all seen it.

Many try to explain their attitude away. They say it is a consequence of low respect for their position, low wages, and the increased chances of meeting an untimely death. Remember one thing. This is America. If you don't want to do a job or it makes you crazy, don't do it!

That is the reason that the question keeps coming up. "Does being a cop make you an asshole, or does the job attract assholes?" Years ago, the subject of an earlier discussion was with me on a trip to a wrestling show in a small town in north Alabama. I was renting them a wrestling ring and my buddy was going to be the referee. During the trip, we had a lot of time on our hands for discussion. He agreed that most cops were in fact, assholes. Since his father was a retired military policeman and was working as a sheriff's deputy, I asked for his input on the question of which came first, the job or the asshole. Since his father was part of the law enforcement establishment, he wanted to believe that it was the job that made them this way.

When we arrived at the high school gym where the wrestling show was to be presented, we immediately went into the locker room. Long hair and beards were prevalent among wrestlers at that time. The high and tight or bald head look was not in vogue yet. The first thing we noticed was one of the regular wrestlers from this promotion who was sporting a new crew cut and wearing mirrored aviator sunglasses (just like mine – the glasses I mean). "What's up?" we asked. He responded,

"I just got a job as an Alabama State Trooper. Now I can drive as fast as I want to and violate human rights, and there ain't a damn thing anybody can do about it!" The evidence is in. At least in this case, the job attracts assholes.

I know this is not scientific but since very little serious research has been done on this subject, this is the only conclusion I can arrive at. It's a curious thing to me. Have you ever noticed that everyone says they are for law and order, yet as a group, most people don't like the police? When you see one when you are out driving, do you immediately slow down before you even look at the speedometer? Most people respond this way. Does it make you nervous when a police car is following you down the street and do you feel a little relieved when he turns off without bothering you? Sometimes you wonder if you did something wrong without realizing it. After all, we are human and prone to moments of in-attention where we might go a little too fast or not come to a complete stop.

One way you can tell if a town is interested in safety or revenue is how they operate their police officers. Since it is illegal to give them ticket quotas, for the number of tickets they are to give out each day, they now have goals. You still get in trouble if you miss your goal, but goals are legal while quotas are not. If you see a town with an empty police car sitting on the side of the road to make you slow down, that town is interested in public safety. If the car is hidden, manned, and equipped with a radar gun, it is revenue they are interested in. If the car just has a camera that is activated by speed or by crossing a line too soon or too late, then the town definitely just wants revenue. Think about it.

Many sanctimonious people say "the only people that complain about the police are those that the police arrest."

150

They usually will accept no explanation that maligns the integrity of the police force in any way. Watch how that attitude changes when either they or someone close to them gets a ticket. The same thing applies when arrested and convicted of more serious crimes. The sanctimonious always say that only the guilty are arrested. When one of them is charged with a crime, there is some kind of mistake or entrapment involved. At least, that is what they would have you believe. Don't get me wrong. Society must have a group of people designated to enforce the rules. Without them, we would have chaos. I just wish they would go about their jobs treating people as innocent until proven guilty as the Constitution requires. I also want them to treat others as they would want to be treated if the roles were reversed. That is not presently the case in America, or anywhere else in the world that I have been.

CHAPTER TWENTY SIX

The Modern Military Mind

At this point the aliens decided we needed to talk about the modern military. As a Vietnam era veteran, I've seen a lot of changes in America when it comes to attitudes concerning America's military. I've worked for the Army, Navy, and Air Force as a civilian for more than 20 years so I have a pretty good insight into their thoughts and actions.

In the old days, it was said that you "went into the service." It was a service you performed for the good of the country. The draft was in full swing as it has been off and on throughout most of our history. During the last years of the draft, service in the military was not seen to be a good thing. We were spit on, called names, and generally disrespected when in uniform. What made it even stranger was that most of the people in the military were forced to be there one way or another. Either they were drafted into the Army or went into another branch of service to avoid being drafted.

We were the same age as most of those calling us names and that made it a lot harder to take. Since most were forced to serve, at little pay and great personal risk, they should have been applauded. Once the draft was eliminated, America's attitude towards those serving gradually changed. Today, everyone talks about the "heroes" who serve. People go up to military members and say, "thank you for your service." Absolutely no one thanked me for my service.

Everyone is aware of the phenomenon where someone who never attended a certain university will practically worship that university and its football team. They really have no connection to that university or football team but still get a vicarious thrill from their success. Many of them are "mouth breathing, bottom feeders" who will fight you if you say anything bad about their team. These fans are generally the type who will jump on the band wagon when a team is winning but often change to worship of another team if they are on a losing streak. A lot of the poorer sort, who have little to nothing going for themselves personally, are the most rabid fans.

Let's consider the United States as a whole. We have lost millions of manufacturing jobs. Our home values are in a downward spiral. Our retirement funds are shrinking (if we are lucky enough to have any). We rank very low among the nations of the world in investment in new infrastructure and in students studying science, technology, engineering, and math. Our quality of life is lower than our parent's generation. America is not number one in every category as it once was.

One place where we are still number one is military might. That number one ranking may just be why people are jumping on the band wagon and singing the praises of the military now. They never served in the military. Their children haven't served and don't plan to serve. Everything else seems to be going badly for America but the American military is number one in military might world-wide. They may have just assumed the role of "America's Team". They are number one so we love them. We don't have much else to be proud of so they are our new heroes. This is just a hypothesis but give it some thought. There is definitely a parallel between worship of sports teams and worship of today's military.

It was another attack of the PC police who demanded that the draft end. Their position was that it targeted the poor to fight for the rich. The point was made that poor folks, many of them minorities, could not afford to go to college to get a draft deferment. That caused more of them to have to go into the service right after high school. The upper classes, mostly white, were at least allowed to defer their service till after getting a college education. This let them be Officers or allowed them more time to come up with other reasons to be excused from service. Once the PC police decided that this situation must change, nothing else would do. In 1973 the Vietnam War was almost over so it seemed like a good time to end the draft. It was obvious to these rocket scientists that once Vietnam was over, there would be no need for a large body of soldiers ever again. Obviously, none of them ever passed a history course.

A direct result of this type of thinking is that today, the actual combat troops that serve mostly in the Army and Marine Corps have been rode hard and put up wet. During Vietnam, we had the draft to supply large numbers of lower ranking service members. Most served a two year tour and then went back to their civilian life. A lot of draftee's served in Vietnam. Most of the people who served in Vietnam were there for about one year. A few people volunteered to stay for a second tour. It was very rare that you met anyone who was there for three tours. If they were there for more than one tour, they probably volunteered. Individual reasons ranged from dedication to our country down to they had "girlfriend

Vietnam". Now look at the last decade of war in the Middle East using an all volunteer force. Most of the actual war fighters have been there for multiple tours. I have heard of many who have been there ten or more times! That means that they have been engaged in combat in a war zone for years. My point is that if we are going to engage in long term wars then we must re-institute the draft to support that action.

How many times can you see your buddy blown up or shot by a sniper who looks just like every other citizen of the country we invaded, before your personality changes to deal with the difficult situation? Anyone who has been in a war zone understands that it is not possible to stay PC when you can't tell the enemy from the friendlies. When you can't trust anyone and you never know when or where you will be attacked, it wears you down. Soon you de-humanize the enemy and the foreign citizens around you so you can deal with the situation.

We send the same soldiers back to the war over and over again because that is all we have to send. To maintain required troop strength in the field we have no choice. The draft provided a constant stream of new troops to send to war. With the operational tempo we have in place today is it any wonder that people suffer from PTSD or snap and commit what the PC police label atrocities? The rising suicide rate among service members is another major problem. Even with today's high levels of overall troop strength we must remember that the percentage of actual combat soldiers available is very small compared to the total. We need a cadre of professionals augmented by a steady stream of draftees. Draftees could be paid less and professionals could be paid a solid middle class wage.

In the old days, because it was a service to the nation, you were paid very little while on active duty. As an E5 on active duty I actually made less money than I received for my college GI Bill after I got out. Since we had a system of compulsory service, pay was very low. To balance this, a very generous retirement system was put in place. At the end of twenty years service, you can retire and immediately begin to receive fifty per cent of your base pay for the rest of your life. Imagine that you go into the military when you are twenty years old. You can retire at forty years of age and receive a retirement check until you die. If you live to the average age for men of seventy five years, that means you will receive fifty per cent of your active duty pay, with cost of living adjustments for the next thirty five years. You can still work another job and receive the retirement pay simultaneously. Add to this veteran's preference in hiring for government jobs and it begins to look pretty sweet these days.

Military retirees have always been pretty crafty when it comes to finding government jobs within the Department of Defense to move into after they retire from active duty. In fact, there was so much chicanery going on that legislation had to be passed making it illegal for a military retiree to go to work for the federal civil service for a minimum of one hundred eighty days from their date of retirement.

That rule was designed to preclude a fairly common practice that you see everywhere today. The wily service member either writes a civilian job description that just happens to require the exact qualifications that he/her has or gets a crony to do it. They then "compete" for the job and get selected by their friends who helped them establish the position. They then put themselves on terminal leave, start the civilian job, and receive military pay and civil service pay for the last month or two of their military obligation. After working as a civilian employee for around two months, they finally officially retire from the military service.

Since a "state of emergency" was declared after the tragic events of 9/11, the requirement to wait one hundred and eighty days has been waived. Since that happened, the percentage of military retirees with Department of Defense jobs has risen astronomically. Don't get me wrong. Not every military retiree does this. It's not because they don't want to do it. It's because most of them have such contempt and disdain for the civilian employees that they never learn how to navigate within the civilian personnel system. In other words, they don't know how!

Without the draft available to fill the manpower needs of the Army and the threat of the draft to fill the other services, increased compensation was required to get people to join the volunteer force. Base pay was substantially increased every year. Housing allowances went ever higher. Specialty pays to entice people to enter hard to fill niches were established. Enlistment bonuses and re-enlistment bonuses went through the roof. It is said that today, the total cost of fielding one service member is $1,000,000 per year. That's a long way from the "short hundred" ($98 after taxes) we received as Privates during the last years of the draft. I'm not saying that the service member makes a million dollars. I am saying that when all costs are considered, it costs about a million dollars to field one service member. What most people don't realize is that about thirty percent of service members "allowances" are non-taxable. If you only consider the base salary, you will think that they don't make much money. Let's consider a married enlisted person who has been promoted to E4 with three years of service. The total salary in 2013 was around $25,480. They also receive $325.04 per month subsistence allowance or what we used to call "separate rations." Housing allowances are added to this. They depend on where you are located and can range from about $700 per month to over $2500 per month. You can live in government supplied quarters instead and then you don't receive this allowance. On the other hand, you don't have to worry about repairs, property taxes, utilities and so on like the average citizen does. Remember that the allowances are non-taxable too. The compensation detailed here does not include the value of free health care, tax free shopping, free and low cost recreation facilities, and a whole lot more. Just the easily identified compensation places the E4 solidly in the middle class.

I hear a lot of uninformed people speaking out about how little our service members make. Most of them don't have a clue to what that actually is. They have memories of the old days when it was a "service" and when you had to sacrifice your financial security to defend America. For a reality check, take a look in the parking lot on any military base with American troops on it. When I served, it was filled with older cars. Many of them were jointly owned by a pool of soldiers. We took turns driving them and shared the expense of required maintenance to keep them running. Today, you rarely see an older car in the lot. It is strange enough that we notice the older cars more than a new car in the lot. I'm talking high dollar cars too. Mercedes, Audi, Cadillac Escalade, and other high end cars are driven by enlisted service members, and not just by officers. Enlisted members now have disposable income for high end car purchases too. When you watch the old war movies and see officers quarters that are real dumps with faulty plumbing and dirt yards, remember one thing. These do not exist anymore. A deep look at military compensation by the Department of Defense revealed that in most cases, today's service member makes from fifteen to thirty five percent more than in a comparable civilian job.

Don't get me wrong. I am a third generation veteran whose wife and son also serve or have served in the military. At some point, this generosity is going to have to be looked at. Our country can't afford to keep increasing military compensation at the rate they have for the past 30 years. Look at what happened to the Soviet Union. They spent too much on "Defense" for too many years. Too much "Defense" spending resulted in their total collapse. In the place of the Soviet Union, today we have a handful of third world countries. Do we want this to happen to us?

The auto industry was almost bankrupted by the generous retirement programs that the unions insisted on. Either salaries must be reined in or a significant adjustment must be made to the military retirement system to make it fair. How do you justify life-long compensation for these people when there is talk of cutting social security payments to the majority of the population? There is open discussion about increasing the age at which you are eligible to receive social security payments based on the fact that humans are living longer. What would be wrong with the military retirement being earned at 20 years service but paid out beginning the same age as social security? If it is fair for one government program that you must pay into in order to qualify for it, then why is it not fair to apply the same standard to military service?

159

Low military pay is no longer a justification for the overly generous retirement plan in place today. Today, low pay for the military is a myth. The retirement plan for our military has not substantially changed in more than thirty years while military pay has skyrocketed. Most large companies offer only a thrift savings plans that the worker contributes to. That is if they offer any retirement program at all. The military offers a very sweet retirement program and a thrift savings plan on top of it.

We need to put "service" back into the equation for figuring military compensation. The position we are in today is untenable.

During the time I was working for the Army as a civilian, it was determined that soldiers should be working in the jobs for which they were trained. This sounds logical to any thinking person. Before this monumental decision, soldiers were used to hand out towels at the gym, cut grass in common areas, and perform a number of other non-military job related functions. They hired some civilians to replace the duty soldiers and returned them all to their units to do what they were trained for. The decision was also made that professional civilians would provide all the recreational support the Army needed. No longer would soldiers have to put on car washes, bake sales and the like in order to finance unit picnics or team sports. We would do it for them. This works amazingly well. When you consider how much it costs for fully trained military people to stay away from their real jobs as they cook hotdogs or perform other menial tasks it is absurd. It is way more cost effective to have professionals do it for them.

Civilian employees are required to come to the job trained and ready to go. Military people are a blank slate upon which the requirements of the service are etched during years of comprehensive training. During my career of support for the military I have worked for the Army, Navy, and Air Force. One thing the Navy and Air Force have in common is their feelings of superiority to the Army. They never miss a chance to tell all who will listen how smart they are and how dumb the Army is. The Army made the decision in the early 1980's to put soldiers in soldier jobs and use civilians to support them in every way possible. In 2014, the Navy still has senior enlisted people out washing cars and cooking hotdogs to raise money to support unit functions. Imagine the cost of six sailors, all in the grade E-7 and above, buying charcoal, securing a grill, shopping for stuff to sell, cooking hotdogs, selling the hotdogs, cleaning up afterwards and so on. It happens almost every week on the base where I used to work. The combined cost of six or more senior enlisted leaders, spending at least half a day each supporting an activity that might yield a hundred dollar profit is ludicrous.

To further compound the insanity, Navy Chiefs (pay grades E-7 thru E-9) are ranked and graded with heavy emphasis on their additional duties with less emphasis on actual job performance. That is to say, the more reasons they can come up with not to perform the duties they are actually trained for, the better they are perceived to be.

I had to sit in on a Chief ranking board and was disturbed to find out what the Navy considers a superior Chief. The Chief in my department was actually performing assigned duties that would normally be performed by a college educated, trained civilian professional. The job grade would be equivalent to O-4 or Lieutenant Commander in the Navy. My Chief (pay grade E-7) was held to be less important and was ranked lower than most of the other Chiefs because he was not involved in as many "collateral duties" such as raising money for MWR events, collecting specimens for urinalysis and so on. His level of actual job responsibility was not recognized at all in ranking the Chiefs. Is this another unintended consequence? Has the Navy put so much emphasis on community involvement and collateral duties that actual duty performance has been forgotten? If this is how these boards operate across the Navy, then we have definitely strayed from reality.

As smart as they are supposed to be, how did they get to this state? By the use of civilian MWR professionals to run their programs and service members being graded by how well they do their actual job, the Army is light years ahead of the Navy. My time spent with the Air Force was similar. Every chance they got, they expounded on how smart they were and how stupid any and all involved with the Army were. I've got news for you. Everything they "discovered" during the year I spent working with Air Force Morale, Welfare, and Recreation (MWR), the Army had done at least ten years before.

I do have to say that the Air Force MWR is also superior to the Navy's. The Air Force was smart enough to add some interesting elements to MWR. Did you know the morgue and dining facilities (not called mess halls like in the old days) are officially part of Air Force MWR? That way when the Air Force goes to war they will always include the finer things of life as "mission essential equipment".

During Desert Storm the Army deployed with no thought to MWR until they had been there for months. They had guys playing a form of baseball with a pair of socks wrapped in tape for a ball and a sawed off broom handle for a bat just to amuse themselves. The Air Force dropped their MWR package the first day. It included inflatable buildings for fully equipped recreation centers. This was only possible because someone thought of making essentials like the morgue and mess halls part of MWR. I have to give credit where credit is due. That was a great idea.

While I never thought I would see the day when the PC police would defend the military services, they are definitely on the job today. Mention in public that you think we should cut defense spending and they will immediately attack you both verbally and sometimes physically. As they used to say, "Nothing is too good for the troops!" When I was on active duty, it was "Nothing is too good, for the troops!" It's the same phrase but with a much different meaning.

Over the decades of working for the different branches of the military, I have developed a level of cynicism when it comes to those defending cuts in military spending. There are so many ways that a rational person could save money without adversely effecting military readiness. There are many people within the government whose jobs seem to consist of making it impossible to do so. Take for example something as simple as the Physical Training (PT) Uniform. It consists of shorts and t-shirt. Why can't all the services have the same shorts and t-shirt? They could use the same style and material and just use different colors. Instead, they each have different shorts and t-shirts that each individual branch of service exhaustively tested over a period of years at a cost of millions of dollars per service.

When I was in school in Physical Education class, we generally wore whatever shorts and t-shirts our mother's bought us. I just can't see how something you will wear for such a short amount of time is worth all the bother. There are plenty of off the shelf shorts and t-shirts that would fill the bill. This is just one example of their insane drive to waste money. The same situation exists with their uniforms.

Every service wants a different type of camouflage uniform. The pockets must be placed differently. The shape of the patterns must be different. The colors must of course, be different. Why not design one uniform and let them buy in different colors? They each justify their wants, not their needs, by saying they are special and must have something special designed just for them. When the Navy designed their new digital uniform they decided that the boots had to have a nine inch leather upper. Most military boots have an eight inch upper. There are numerous brands of boots with eight inch uppers that are approved for use with military uniforms. The Navy specified a non-standard, nine inch upper. The result was that the Navy approved boot wasn't comfortable and actually rubbed the wearer raw on the back of the calf. That is because a nine inch leather upper ends in the middle of the calf muscle and not just under it as the eight inch boot does.

Besides being uncomfortable, they are more expensive. I have seen Navy personnel with the new boots and personally examined them. The company providing them took standard boots with an eight inch leather upper and sewed another inch of leather to them to achieve the nine inch upper standard required by the Navy. With either boot design, you cannot see the top of the boot because it is under the bloused trouser leg. There is no legitimate reason for the Navy to have specified a nine inch leather upper. This is the kind of thinking that pervades the military and the government in general.

Many people have heard of the $500 hammer or the $900 toilet seats ordered by the government. Most people have heard about this and are totally flabbergasted. You can go to almost any hardware store and get a great hammer for $10 to $20. They have no idea how this could happen. Stand by while I tell you.

Most of the contracting officers within the government have to work from a huge document called the "FAR" or *Federal Acquisitions Regulation*. They are given strict guidelines on every aspect of purchasing. They are told about who you can order from, what you can pay for each item, set aside programs to correct PC transgressions of the past and a whole lot more. They are taught not to question the specifications that are listed as essential by the person or persons placing the order. They must order items that conform to those specifications. They are not allowed to use their initiative.

In the case of the $500 hammer, it probably went something like this. Someone needed some hammers so they prepared a requisition to order same. Under the specifications section, they described what they thought was a regular old, run of the mill hammer. They described the weight of the hammer head, the length of the handle, maybe something about whether it was wood or fiberglass and so on. The question is then, what makes up the specifications for a "regular old hammer". Chances are the specifications listed on the order listed something that was not really "regular". Maybe they specified a seventeen ounce hammer head or a twelve and a half inch long handle made of oak or some other specific wood material. When the contracting officer sends the item out for bids, the company that responds must bid on providing a hammer that meets the specifications listed on the bid sheet. If the specifications are considered "non-standard", the bidder is allowed to add on developmental costs and design costs and

165

even equipment costs to allow them to provide the non-standard item. They also get to add project management costs and profit to the bid. When you add it all together, you get a $10 hammer that costs $500. This happens a lot more often than most people think. Everyone involved is just following the rules. Common sense need not apply.

On a much higher end scale, the services each want to be pre-eminent among the services. The Air Force has already staked the claim to outer space. A lot of people have forgotten or never knew that the Air Force began life as the Army Air Corps. It was just another element of the Army like Infantry, Artillery, Armor, etc.

Just after the Air Force was created, they brokered a plan that said that they could have armed aircraft and the Army could not. They already had competition for resources from the Navy and the Marine Corps. The Army had to sneak its way into arming helicopters that became such an integral part of the consciousness during Vietnam. As a child whose family was stationed at Fort Rucker, Alabama, I got to watch the development of the helicopter as a true war machine. They added machine guns and rocket launchers, perfecting the machines and the tactics they would use before the Air Force caught on.

The Air Force wants to be in the rear with the gear and destroy all targets from twenty miles out (or more). One of the best air-to-ground support aircraft ever developed is the A-10 Warthog. It is a tank buster unrivaled in history. Its only drawback is that it requires the pilot to get in close. That is definitely not in the Air Forces long term plans. They like to fly fast and shoot from far away. Close air support for troops on the ground is the very last thing on their mind. They have been trying to dump the Warthog from their inventory for more than twenty years. It is just not sexy enough to fit their self image. They want to spend trillions of dollars developing new aircraft to fight an enemy that does not exist today. Our aircraft are the best in the world already. Who will we fight that requires us to have even better, faster, more expensive planes than we do now?

Take a look at the Air Force F-22 fighter. It does have a cool name, "Raptor" but that is the only cool thing about it. The Raptor was first conceived in the 80's, while the Cold War with the Soviets was still active. We wanted something that could beat the expected new generation of Soviet fighters in a dogfight. When the Soviet Union collapsed due to excessive military spending, we did not need the F-22. Logic says that the program would then die.

The Air Force wanted a new toy anyway. They lined up their Congressional lobbyist's and rammed through a spending bill to finance their scheme. The Generals then tried to out-do each other with attaching more and more hi-tech gadgets to the plane. The Raptor became a vehicle to carry a virtual laundry list of technologies. For every design change to embrace a new technology there was an increase in cost. The Raptor was originally to cost about $139,000,000 each but mushroomed to around $412,000,000 each. The original plan was to purchase six hundred and forty eight Raptors but the purchase was cut off at one hundred and eighty eight planes.

The price is horrible but it gets worse. For every hour of flight time, the Raptor requires about forty five hours of maintenance. It takes about three thousand people just to keep up with this requirement. This supposedly wonderful, state of the art fighter jet was not used in Iraq, Afghanistan, or in any other war zone. The entire fleet of Raptors has been grounded due to safety considerations. As a jobs program, this would be a wonderful investment if it didn't cost so much. As an effective use of government money to construct a usable war fighting machine, it is incredibly wasteful.

You hear a lot of talk from the Navy about needing more aircraft carriers. Around the Navy it is said that during any meeting attended by Admirals, they talk ninety five percent of the time about their "toys" and only five percent about their "boys". I predict that they will try to justify more carriers. It won't be because there is a legitimate "need." The decision will be based on the Admirals' desire for more "toys". Members of Congress like the economic impact on their community if they get the contract to build one. The economic impact of having an aircraft carrier stationed in your congressional district is huge as well.

Imagine around five thousand well paid sailors living and spending in your local community. Add to that the thousands of support jobs required to keep the five thousand sailors living and ready to go to sea. A carrier effects housing, schools, local police forces, fast food and any other kind of business you can think of. Gaining or losing a carrier can mean the difference in a vital community or a declining one. If I was going to bet, the future fate of the carrier force depends more on the clout of individual congressmen and their ability to land projects for their constituents. The actual needs of the maritime strategy are a distant consideration. Not long ago the Navy conducted a training exercise where Navy Admirals commanding a Task Force built around aircraft carriers were attacked by irregular forces commanded by a retired Marine Corps General. The irregular force inflicted severe casualties on the Navy. In laymen's terms, the Admiral's got their butts kicked. Aircraft carriers are great for conventional warfare but we are facing unconventional enemies today. There has to be a change in the maritime strategy.

Of all the American Armed Forces, the United States Navy has to be the one most rooted in tradition. They copied the English Navy right down the line and maintain those traditions today. There was a rigid social caste system in England and that pattern was followed in their Navy. As mentioned earlier, many of the seamen in the old English Navy were forced into service against their will. If volunteers were not available, then press gangs went out and captured enough men to man the ships. Common sailors were kept in the worst of conditions and it was expected and accepted by all. The petty officers served as a bulwark between the lower ranks and the officers. When a person somehow elevated himself to the rank of petty officer or more rarely, commissioned officer rank, they stubbornly maintained that structured society. You would think that they would try to make things better since they had lived in those conditions.

The United States Navy loves tradition because it gives them an excuse for all types of otherwise irrational activities. Take for example the protracted initiation into the fraternity of Navy Chiefs. All over the Navy, there is a six week program of initiation into the "Goat Locker". They get up early and run together and do other types of activities that would appear to the average outsider to be fraternity bull shit. This includes washing cars, serving doughnuts, raising money for projects and so on. Don't forget that we are paying them the whole time they participate in these activities. Not only are we paying them, we are paying the Chiefs who are supervising these antics as well. None of them are doing anything remotely related to the job we hired and trained them for during this period. This period of initiation culminates with a free trip to the USS Constitution for many of them where they get to spend the night on board. How much does all this cost?

Once they become Chief's they act like "want-to-be" Officers. They wear the same uniform (different insignia); have the Chief's Mess to mirror the Officer's Mess and so on. This fraternity mentality extends to how the chiefs performance is rated during their career. One of the measurements is how active you are within the chief's mess. Being Army trained, it is hard for me to stomach all this nonsense. We are trained to lead from the front. That means leadership by example, not literally from in the front. We take care of the troops first. When we go into the mess hall to eat, we make sure all our people have something to eat and then we get something. I never saw this with the Navy. They may have a separate enlisted mess, Chief's Mess, Officer's Mess, Captain's Mess, and Admiral's Mess (if there is one around). Mess stewards, white table cloth dining, and special menus make sure you understand the difference in the social status of each group.

In the Army mess hall, the commander may have a table at the end of the room but everyone else sits where they want to and they all eat from the same chow line. There are no special menus based on rank.

Somehow, lobbyists for the Navy have convinced Congress that many Navy Officers should make more money than the approved pay scale dictates. Many make $30,000 bonuses for each year they serve. Pilots make a huge yearly bonus whether they are actively flying or not. They just have to maintain their flight physical. I know of some officers who are receiving this annual bonus and haven't served in aviation for years! If that wasn't bad enough, Naval Flight Officers (NFO) are also paid these bonuses. NFO's are people who wanted to be pilots but couldn't qualify for one reason or another. They are laughingly referred to as Non Flying Objects by the rest of the Navy yet they too receive bonuses around $30,000 per year. I personally know a Non Flying Object who hasn't served in Navy Aviation for more than five years and will never go back there, yet he still receives the bonus bucks. Aviation gave him to Recruiting because they didn't want him anymore. If he was valuable to Aviation, they would have kept him to start with or asked for him back after a short tour in Recruiting. Why is he still allowed to draw the bonus?

A lot of people still think that it's like it was back when "An Officer and a Gentleman" was made. They want to think that Naval Aviators can't wait to get off Active Duty and take their pilot skills to the airlines where they will earn big bucks forever after. The fact is, the airlines don't routinely pay more than the Navy does. A lot of the routes that civilian pilots fly for the airlines pay less than $30,000 per year. For the most part, Naval Aviators have to be forced to leave the Navy now. They stay in the Navy just as long as the government will let them stay. That in turn causes a glut of higher ranking pilots on Active Duty. You have Officers performing jobs that used to be held by lower ranking Officers because you just don't have anything else to do with them. That's an eye opener!

Submarine Officers get their bonus whether on a tour on a submarine or on a shore tour. As long as they are slated to return to Submarine service sometime in the future, they continue to receive their bonus. That does make a little more sense than the aviation field. These are just two examples of what should fall under the catch all "Fraud, Waste, and Abuse". Why do they continue to get specialty pay when they are not performing the specialty? When people talk about military compensation, most speak from a position of total ignorance.

Since I'm talking about Submarines I will tell you another weird idea the Navy has. During World War II when it was absolutely essential that we keep as many ships and submarines in action as possible they went about a maintenance refit like this. The submarine crew would deliver their sub to a specific shipyard. The whole crew would then move to another sub and go back to sea. That kept a well trained crew together and in action.

Today they leave the crew assigned to the submarine during its maintenance refit. This can take up to two years. During this time, the crew has to go ashore and use simulators to try to keep their skills current. The Officers supervise as a team of civilians actually perform the maintenance. This causes degradation of the crew's skills, low morale, and has ended the submarine career of many valuable sailors. Remember that the sailors who are selected for submarine service are the best and the brightest the United States has to offer. They have to be to operate the highly technical Nuclear submarines and their weapons systems. It is criminal to waste valuable resources like that when they had a tried and proven system that helped us win World War II. Let the shipyard professionals deal with the maintenance and keep the Officers and crews together and engaged at sea.

Another overlooked military problem is "grade creep". It is a fact that there are more general and flag officers serving today than ever before. Just look at the ratios of general and flag officers to other troops over the years:

172

- August 1945: 1 to 6,000 World War II
- September 1967: 1 to 2,615 Vietnam War
- March 2010: 1 to 1,489

During World War II the ratio of Officers to Enlisted was about one Officer to ten Enlisted. Today it is closer to one Officer to six Enlisted. Do today's service members need more supervision than in past years? Are today's service members harder to manage and require more leadership than service members during the Draft?

If you look at all ranks, there are more people in higher ranks than ever before. Is this because the pay and benefits are so good that more people want to stay in than we really need in the upper ranks? If life in the military is so hard, why do so many want to stay there until made to leave?

The fact is that we could still have a strong national defense if we significantly cut defense spending. The military leaders decide where the cuts will come from within their branch of service. All of them cut things that will create the shrillest outcry from those affected by the cuts. The leaders want the cuts to hurt people because people complain. That keeps the attention of those that don't know any better on the wrong issue. The leaders want to keep all their toys and pet projects intact.

Again, my father served in the Air force. I served in the Army. My wife served in the Army and Army Reserve. My brother served in the Army Reserve. My son is a Navy Officer. I've worked as a civilian employee of the Army, Navy, and Air Force. I am proud of that service. I am not anti-military. I am just reporting the facts so that people will begin to think for

173

themselves. With so few Americans actually serving today, there is a wealth of misinformation around. Everyone should base their actions and opinions on facts and not emotions. Think about it.

CHAPTER TWENTY SEVEN

Government Managers

Government managers are taught from the first day on the job to spend every penny they can. If you can execute one hundred percent of your budget every year, and always ask for more, then you are seen as being a great manager. When you create your annual budget, you are usually instructed to simply add at least ten percent to the amount you spent last year. If you can come up with justification for more spending, that is even better.

This should have been a clue to me that I was "different." In spite of direction from leadership, I absolutely refused to spend money on anything that was not needed to do the job. As each year came to an end, I would notify my nominal superiors of this year's savings and when I prepared my budget for the coming year, I often asked for less than the year before. Some of them looked at me as if I was touched in the head. How did I plan to succeed in a government job if I would not increase my spending each and every year?

One of the most wasteful examples of this ever seen was at an Army base where I worked. The base Financial Manager had an open contract with an asphalt paving company. The last week of each fiscal year he would dump every available penny into that paving contract so that he could show one hundred percent budget execution year after year. He was highly praised for this and got huge bonuses for doing a great job. The problem was they paved dirt roads to nowhere. Anyone with a brain understands that there is a limit to how much paving you need to do on a base that hadn't built a new road in fifty years or more.

He performed other financial magic as well. When there was a ban on money for new construction, and the post commander wanted a new welcome center, he just had the old building demolished down to the foundation. He then directed the use of maintenance funds to renovate the old building. This may have been technically legal but was definitely not the intent of Congress when they froze construction funding.

Navy Recruiting Command used a variation of the open contract for paving that the Army base used. Their "open contract" was with our contracted advertising agency. At budget time they would show that they cut the advertising budget by millions of dollars. Everyone was happy because the Navy was admitting that because of the state of the economy, they really didn't have to spend much to get all the recruits they needed. During the last few days of the fiscal year they would give all the left over money, usually millions, to Navy Advertising because they could quickly spend it through their advertising agency. That allowed the Navy to get pats on the back for cutting the advertising budget and still allowed them to show their television commercials using money that should have been turned back into the Treasury. One hundred percent budget execution wins again! Multiply this behavior through all departments of government and you will see that there is plenty of room for cuts without hurting Defense or any other department.

Congress probably gets a lot of complaints from the civilian world when the civilians see the quality of the recreation facilities on most military bases. Just a few years ago, tax dollars were routinely used to support golf courses, the club system, liquor stores and so on. Congress finally ruled that these recreation activities had to become self supporting. For years they would make a rule and the military would achieve a backdoor work-a-round. They would buy most things with funds generated by the facility but would build the facility with tax dollars. They might also pay the utilities, maintenance bill or pay the worker's salaries and so on with tax dollars. Finally, Congress put a stop to it totally. Once no tax dollar could be used to support these facilities, many of them closed up. They just could not be operated on a cost effective basis while following government rules.

One of the boondoggles used to try to get around this played out at Fort McClellan, Alabama. We were in the heart of the seven year drought cycle. The appearance of the golf course was suffering due to lack of rain. Someone decided that an irrigation system should be installed with sprinklers covering the entire eighteen hole course. The initial cost estimate was so high that the project could not be approved at post level. Remember that no tax dollars could be spent to support a golf course at that time. It was decided that locally generated funds would buy the material needed to irrigate the golf course.

The local Army Engineer Company would install the system as a training exercise. They had a lot of fun driving around in our golf carts, generally caused a lot of un-needed destruction, and failed miserably in their attempt to make the system work. Finally, after more than a year of trying, it was decided that we could hire someone to repair the irrigation system without having to go higher for approval. Guess what? It cost more to dig up the unworkable system and fix it than the original estimate for new construction of a lock and key system.

Another golf related boondoggle occurred when the General commanding the Fort decided that he really needed to be able to hit a bucket of balls – any time, day or night. To hit golf balls at night requires a very expensive lighting system as well as using a lot of electricity. Somehow, he always knew how to turn on the lights but rarely remembered to turn them off.

No tax dollars were to be used to support the golf course. It was supposed to be a totally self sufficient operation. The General directed the post engineers to install lights on the golf course driving range so that he could "exercise" at night. He was much too busy any other time but his health and well being would suffer without this particular exercise opportunity. Sports activities that supported fitness are allowed to be supported with tax dollars. Golf courses are specifically excluded. The Engineers had no choice but to comply as the General was the ultimate authority on the Fort. Everyone knew it was wrong but who will tell the Emperor that he has no clothes?

During the 90's, the government came up with a great idea to save money. They would close or consolidate military bases that were not cost effective to operate. They would avoid duplication of efforts and keep operations in low cost areas instead of high cost ones. That was the plan but the execution was far different. Let's go back to Fort McClellan for example. With all its faults and devious financial moves, it was still judged to be the most cost effective base in TRADOC. To reward our frugal ways, a bonus of one million dollars was given to us to spend on Quality of Life initiatives. The following year Fort McClellan was put on the Base Closure list as being inefficient and the most expendable base in TRADOC.

Did I mention that Fort McClellan was the home of the only live agent chemical training facility in the free world? Did I mention that other communities did not want the live agent training facility in their neighborhood and would not grant the required permits to build a new one? The one thing we had going against us was that the state of Alabama voted Republican in the Presidential election and the Democrat won. Many of the assets from Fort McClellan went to states that voted Democrat. It appeared that we were being punished for voting the wrong way. For more than three years after the base was officially closed, new construction projects were still being worked on. The contracts had already been issued so the work went on as scheduled.

There is much waste in other areas as well. During the Hurricane Katrina fiasco, the property previously known as Fort McClellan was considered as a refuge for families displaced by the disaster. At one time we had over twelve hundred hotel style rooms constructed. These were designed to house visiting students attending the various Military Police and Chemical Corps training programs on base. Before their construction, we often contracted for over ninety percent of the hotel rooms in the entire county to house visiting students. Once the base was closed, these buildings stood there empty. In the weeks after Hurricane Katrina struck New Orleans, the government was looking for places to house some of the unfortunates. Someone on the redevelopment board at the property formerly known as "Fort McClellan" graciously offered the use of a battalion sized, starship cluster for their use.

The starship cluster has several floors of open bay barracks, with some administrative offices on the ground floor. There are no elevators, just stairs to reach the upper floors. The stairs are part of the plan to get the basic trainees in shape as they run up and down from their open bays to the battalion assembly area. There is also room on the ground floor for the whole battalion to stand in formation out of the rain.

While this is a great design for basic training, it is a terrible design to house families. Over a million dollars were spent to build temporary plywood walls to divide up the open bay area into family sized quarters. Hundreds of local volunteers came and cleaned up and landscaped the surrounding area. Some families were given the opportunity to move in but they took one look and declined. They were much better off in a hotel paid for by the government.

My observation is this. Why spend the money to convert a starship cluster when I knew there were hundreds of rooms available in other buildings that could have been used with very little cost or effort. I truly believe that the redevelopment people didn't want any refugees on their private reserve but they did want to appear to support the plight of the poor unfortunates.

Speaking of appearances, there was a railroad spur line that entered Fort McClellan and continued by the golf course to a warehouse area. Anyone who wanted to develop industry on the property would welcome the use of low cost rail transportation for their products. The first thing the redevelopment board did was have the tracks taken up. They didn't want the noise and pollution from a train destroying their view of the golf course.

They also allowed many sets of quarters to degrade into an unusable state because they didn't want that class of people living near them. If they could have gotten away with it, they would have made the whole place a gated community for the upper crust. The main achievement of the various redevelopment efforts there was to keep themselves employed and to keep out anything that might disturb their idyllic surroundings.

With all the bases that were closed across America, imagine this attitude applied across the board and the lost opportunities this represents. Housing wasted, job creation averted, jobs lost, crushed hopes and dreams were the results of another cost saving scam on the part of the government. They started with the noble idea of consolidating bases and saving money. In most cases they ended up just transferring the cost to another location and crushing the life out of the community that lost the base.

These are a few examples of your government in action. Multiply this kind of thinking across the Army, Navy, Air Force, Marine Corps, National Guard, plus all other government agencies and see how much waste bordering on fraud there is. I know it sounds like I am picking on the military but that is the area of government I am most familiar with. I have no doubt that egregious events occur all over the government where tax money is wasted on pork barrel projects. We need to be able to trust that those people in government who spend our tax dollars do so wisely. My experience tells me that there must be a fundamental change in management

181

philosophy if we want to get America going in the right direction.

CHAPTER TWENTY EIGHT

The Evolution of Television

My life can be measured by changes in television programming. In the beginning, there were only wholesome, family shows on the three basic channels available. They all had some morning and afternoon kid's shows on as well as a full line of game shows and soap operas. There were also a lot of variety shows in prime time as well. Who could forget watching everything from clowns to dancing bears to Elvis and the Beatles on *The Ed Sullivan Show?* Most channels went off the air around midnight. I still remember the soft background hum as the test pattern with the silhouette of the Indian appeared nightly. Show sponsors were intimately involved with programming. If the sponsor didn't like it, it didn't appear.

There was an army of censors on every set. Some censors represented the sponsor. Some represented the League of Decency or other precursors to the PC police of today. The title of a show often included the sponsor like the *Dinah Shore Chevy Show.* Every September it was a big deal to see the debut of the new car models. They would have them on TV all covered up and on the agreed upon day, all would be revealed. The auto showrooms at the dealers did the same thing. It was a great time.

There seemed to be a lot of westerns on TV then also. The westerns of the day all had horses that could run forever without getting tired, clothes that never got dirty, and guns that never ran out of bullets. Most people don't realize it but many of the early westerns were actually the serials that you used to watch every Saturday at the movie. Cowboy star Lash LaRue made a fortune from TV when he bought the rights to his serialized westerns and sold them to television. He also made sure he signed up for a piece of the pie on merchandising. The King of the Cowboys, Roy Rogers, was not such a shrewd business man. At the height of his popularity, he was a contract player who never shared in the fortune made from merchandizing Roy Roger's memorabilia. He got a lot of free samples but others made millions on lunchboxes, gun and holster sets and so on.

Remember the days when the trip to the movie included the featured movie, at least one cartoon, a newsreel, and a serial of some sort. Serials ranged from westerns to science fiction. Of course a lot of the science fiction back then was really a western without horses and with weird costumes. Back then, all the cigarette companies sponsored shows. It is strange now to think of Granny and Jed Clampett from *The Beverly Hillbillies* appearing at the end of the show lighting up a Winston and singing "Winston tastes good like a cigarette should." The PC police put an end to the cigarette companies advertising on television so that radically changed the entertainment line-up available.

Without that major source of sponsorship money, the shows offered became ever more similar to each other. When a show like *Friends* premiered, there were similar shows on every network. Most people forgot about the others because *Friends* had the best theme song. If you don't believe that theme music is important, try to think of even one long lasting show that does not have a good theme. On the flip side, every *Star Trek* spin-off was wildly accepted and lasted for years except the last one. They deviated from the tried and true *Star Trek* music and the show never caught on. I watched a few episodes and it was actually a good show. The theme music was so different that it alienated the viewer base of devoted *Star Trek* fans.

Every conceivable dish washing and laundry detergent sponsored daytime shows. This coined the phrase "soap opera". The longest running soap opera actually began on radio in 1937. *The Guiding Light* came to television in 1952 and ran continuously until 2009. *As the World Turns* came to television in 1956 and ran until 2010. It's hard to imagine a television show lasting more than fifty years but both of these did.

Kid's shows were different back then too. We watched national programs like *Captain Kangaroo* and *The Howdy Doody Show*. Captain Kangaroo was played by Bob Keeshan. He got his start as Clarabell the clown on *Howdy Doody*. These shows always had a message. Listen to your teachers, be good little boys and girls, always use your blunt nose scissors when making paper dolls and so on.

Local television also provided great kids shows. These usually featured a host like Cousin Cliff Holman who would do some simple magic tricks as he entertained the studio audience made up of local children. I was a 'birthday boy" on *The Cousin Cliff Show* on my fifth birthday. That meant I got to sit in the front row and received a birthday cake live on TV. I also got to reach into the fish bowl filled with pennies. You got to keep all the pennies you could pick up in one hand. I know a handful of pennies picked up by a five year old don't sound like much, but I was proud of those pennies and kept them for a long time. Another feature of local kid's shows was the cartoons. Cousin Cliff always had Popeye cartoons. The other kid's shows had something different. Your loyalty to one show or another was dictated by the cartoons they used.

Cartoons themselves went through a number of changes at the dictate of the PC police. Remember when Wiley Coyote always got blown up or crushed as he tried in vain to catch the Road Runner? There was a period of time when the PC police thought these classic cartoons were too violent. They had them butchered to remove everything they felt was offensive. What was left was unwatchable. After a few years the attention of the PC police was elsewhere and the original cartoons made a comeback.

Not long ago I decided that it would be fun to watch some Saturday morning cartoons and think of that kinder, gentler time. To my amazement, the classics were nowhere to be found. Bugs Bunny, Road Runner, Mighty Mouse, Sylvester and Tweety Bird, and all the rest are gone. I won't even attempt to describe my dismay when I saw what has replaced them. The shows are so PC that you might believe that there is an African-American kid, Asian kid, Hispanic kid, and unidentifiable kid in every group of children. Apparently, they can all dance and sing too.

I'm constantly amazed at the evolution of prime time television over the years. Back when *I Love Lucy* was a prime time favorite, every time Lucy and Desi had a scene in the bedroom, there were twin beds, separated by a night stand. Lucy and Desi both wore pajamas with long sleeves and they were buttoned up to the neck. Today's bedroom scenes would have been considered pornography by the standards of that day.

There were no offensive commercials played either. You never had to sit through an erectile dysfunction or feminine hygiene product commercial while eating your dinner and watching TV back then. Today, it seems like there are very few taboos.

Just a few years ago I watched the infamous *Southpark* episode where they set the television record for saying "shit" the most times in history on a thirty minute show. They said the word one hundred and sixty two times and wrote it another thirty eight times for a total of two hundred utterances in thirty minutes. In the other direction, during the early 90's the envelope pushing show *In Living Color* used a lot of colorful language. Recently the show has been in syndication with most of the colorful language bleeped out. It's hard to believe television censors today are more restrictive than they were in 1991. The question must be asked: Is television shaping the moral values of the people or are the changing morals of the people changing what is acceptable on TV?

CHAPTER TWENTY NINE

General Observations

My conversation with the aliens seemed to be all over the board. We talked about history, television, current events and a lot more. I wanted something tangible and recent to discuss. The aliens asked me what I thought about ethanol. This stopped me cold. I never really gave it much thought yet the aliens felt it was an important development with a lot of unintended consequences.

Everyone knows that farmers have raised corn for years. It can be eaten by humans and by a variety of livestock. You can eat it on the cob, take the corn off the cob and eat it whole, turn it into mush slightly resembling corn and you can convert it into meal. This is used for cornbread and corn muffins. Cattle eat it much the same way. It can even be harvested with the corn stalk and the whole thing ground up and fed to cattle. This was the basic use for corn for centuries.

Everyone has heard that the supply of oil is limited on earth. At the urging of the PC police, scientists came up with the concept of ethanol. In America, it is produced primarily from corn and is used to stretch gasoline supplies. The PC police got laws passed that allow/require ten percent ethanol in most places to be added to your gasoline. In a few places, twenty percent ethanol is acceptable.

That is when the unintended consequences began. Since ethanol is largely alcohol, it will rapidly deteriorate many types of plastic. A lot of the parts developed for the fuel systems in cars, tractors, lawn mowers, chain saws and so on were made of plastic. Use of gasoline with ethanol made these parts disintegrate rendering these devices inoperative. As time passed, these problems were solved by the development of new types of plastics that did not react adversely to alcohol in gasoline. As acceptance of ethanol increased, more and more corn was required to keep up with demand.

I have to note here that corn is not the only source of ethanol. It is just the primary source that America has chosen to use. In Brazil, sugarcane is the primary agricultural product used in ethanol production. While there is very little agreement about how much this has affected food prices, the aliens tend to believe that it has had a tremendous inflationary impact. Increased use of ethanol increased the demand for corn to make it with. The price of corn goes up because of increased demand. That is simple economics.

Corn is also used for food for humans and cattle. If we eat corn, we now pay more for it. If cattle eat corn or corn products, that cost more, we end up paying more for that meat than before. PC gasoline mixed with ethanol costs more because of the addition of this environmentally clean additive, and then the farmer pays more to till his soil. The increased cost of producing the corn is passed on in an ever increasing upward spiral. The companies who transport our food have increased transportation costs because fuel costs more. PC police counter, that gasoline would cost even more if it were not stretched with ethanol. They refuse to believe that increased demand has increased the price of corn or that anything other than cleaner burning gasoline is a consideration.

This is one of those issues where you can't be sure who is telling the truth. Everyone involved has an agenda and will protect that agenda at all costs. The old saying is that figures lie and liars figure. There is a lot of truth in that. This whole debate reminds me of the glory days of Glasnost when the communist hoard was the only enemy worth mentioning. The United States and Russia each had a car entered in a two car race. The car from the United States won the race. As the Soviet version of the PC police reported it, the glorious Soviet race car came in second while the decadent American car came in next to last. It's all a matter of perspective.

With all the problems the aliens brought up I had to agree with them that maybe some kind of adjustment was needed. I personally wasn't ready to see the whole human race wiped out to begin a do-over though. Sure, we humans had made a lot mistakes but there was always a chance that we would do better in the future. When my thoughts on this subject reached the aliens, the high pitched tone that I recognized as laughter filled the room. They thought I was making a joke! Once they saw I was serious they got right to the point. Humans just don't get it.

Humans have been making the same mistakes over and over. Their whole history is cyclical in nature. Civilizations rise and fall. Empires rise and fall. A people rise to the top and dominate the rest of the world only to face inevitable decline. What has changed is the rate at which these cycles occur.

Back when there was no modern communication devices, telephone, telegraph, radio, television, and definitely no internet, things happened at a much slower pace. The Egyptians ruled for several thousand years. Their whole way of life was based on the worship of numerous gods and their economic system was based on slavery. They conquered everyone around them and bent them to their will. Their gods were superior because they were winners.

As far as the people were concerned, if they attacked someone and won, then it must be because the gods were on their side and they were therefore in the right. If they lost an occasional battle, they figured that the gods required an additional sacrifice to make things right. After all, when old Og the Caveman created religion, he made sure that everyone knew that since god was infallible, if anything went wrong, it must be your fault. Maybe your sacrifices were too small or your belief was too weak. No matter what, it is always your fault and not gods. This is a universal truth and holds sway in all religions.

The empire that was Egypt slowly grew until it ruled most of the civilized world of that era. Its power slowly grew and then it slowly declined over a period of centuries.

The Greeks under Alexander the Great set out to conquer the known world. They grew to rule over vast areas of the world but really had no basis for long term rule of those they conquered. Once he was dead it was all over. In most cases, the conquered simply absorbed the conquerors.

Genghis Khan gathered the Mongol tribes together and conquered a vast portion of the known world. They were really limited by their ability to communicate within the ruled area. Because it took so long to send information from one part of the empire to another, often questions and problems were overcome by events before they received an answer from the central government. Lack of speedy communication led to their eventual downfall.

The Ottoman Turks ruled the Mideast for several centuries. For a considerable period the Spanish were on top. Then there was a period when "the sun never set on the British Empire". The United States was a third rate country with a lot of potential until after World War I. We really didn't ascend to the throne of being the world's top dog until World War II was over.

Notice one thing about all these groups that were on top. Their stay at the top keeps getting shorter as the speed of communication gets faster. Communication in today's world is practically instantaneous. There was a golden period when the United States was the leader in every category. We led the way in industrial production and the space race. We had the best quality of life and so on. American products set the standard for quality worldwide. While the race to space was neck and neck with the Russians for a few years, we ultimately won that competition. We created the first space station and were the first humans (that we know of) to set foot on the moon.

In just a very few years our position has slipped in all these areas. Even in space. Our government recently started contracting with the Russians to fly supplies to the international space station. They hope that private companies will assume the burden of the space race. Only a few years ago it was illegal for a private citizen to build or own his own rocket capable of going into space. In spite of this overall degradation of our global position, most Americans still believe that we are on top of the world in every category.

Today we are number one in military strength yet we do not have the will to use it to our advantage. We constantly interfere in the internal politics of smaller nations as if our military position entitles us to dictate the values of everyone else in the world. That is a troubling aspect of being American. Most Americans seem to believe that American democracy is the perfect government and fits the needs of every country. Unfortunately for us and for the world, this is not so.

I have had the benefit of traveling to several mid-eastern countries. These include Saudi Arabia, Bahrain, Kuwait, and Turkey. I spent a lot of time in each of these talking to the regular people. Most Americans can't differentiate between a government and a people.

What I came to understand is that most of the people of the world want a predictable life in which they understand the rules and live by them. It is immaterial to them whether they have a democracy or theocracy or dictatorship as long as they have food, water, electricity, and some modern conveniences. The most important thing they want is to feel safe. To feel safe they need to understand the rules so they can play by them.

While a lot of Americans kept to their circle of American friends, I spent as much time as I could among the local people. Even though the poverty was pervasive, everyone knew their place in society. They knew what was expected of them and exactly where they fit in their social order.

Turkish men spend a lot of time talking, drinking tea and watching the world go by. In the afternoon, I would sit and drink tea with them. On the corner near our favorite spot, there was a young shoe-shine boy plying his trade. He was about six years old and he smoked to stave off the hunger pangs as he waited to shine some shoes. He hoped that some Americans would stop by for a shine because they always paid him more than the Turkish grownups. As the day went on the small boy shined an American's shoes and the boys eyes lit up as he contemplated the meal he would now be able to afford. Just after the American left, a seven or eight year old shoe shine boy came up and took the boys money and said it was now his corner. The smaller boy wiped away the tears as he walked away. Later, the same thing happened to that shoe shine boy as an even older boy wanted the corner for his shoe shine business. All the time the adult Turks were watching and laughing about this. No one came to the aid of the younger boys. I finally had to ask why they let this happen. Their answer was "Inshallah". It is the will of God. The boys must learn to fend for themselves. How else would they become a man? To an American this sounds unduly harsh yet to them it is an acceptable way of life. They understand the situation and adapt to it.

I spent some time with a Turkish family while working for the Air Force as a civilian at Incirlik, Turkey. The daughter of the family worked for the Americans at the base. She was a beautiful thirty year old virgin who lived in a compound in Adana with generations of her family. Although she had a college education and had briefly taught English at the university, she found that she could make more money working for the Americans as a clerk on the base. Of course most of her money went straight to her father so he was very proud of her good fortune to have a job with the Americans. When she accompanied me as a tour guide on trips to Adana, we were always accompanied by members of her family. Because I was much older than her I was treated like an "uncle." However, at no time was I ever allowed to be alone with any of their female family members. She could not be with me unaccompanied, even in a public place.

On one trip I treated the group to lunch at MacDonald's. To Americans this doesn't seem like a big deal. In the mideast, a trip to MacDonald's is a special event. You might see a parking lot filled with Mercedes and even the occasional Rolls. Inside you will find a hostess with a clipboard making reservations for parties and other group gatherings as if MacDonald's was fine dining. For the average Turk, the cost is prohibitive. Even a lowly Happy Meal costs about five dollars or more. When you consider that many adult males work six days per week, twelve to fourteen hours per day for forty to fifty dollars while females receive even less, then you begin to understand why a trip to MacDonald's is such a big deal.

We sat outside with a short fence between us and a large open park. There were at least fifty small boys standing close by smoking cigarettes and staring at us and our food. With typical American lack of understanding I gave a handful of small Turkish bills to one of the particularly hungry looking children. I might have given him two or three dollars worth of Turkish bills and hoped he would be able to get a meal from a Turkish vendor. I had already discovered that if I purchased lunch for my Turkish friends, it always cost five to ten times as much as if they bought it.

A couple of the guys who helped me out as interpreters and local guides could buy chicken tava with unleavened bread with two forks for one dollar American. With the bread included, it was enough for the two of them to have a belly filling meal. If I bought it myself, it was at least five dollars but sometimes even more.

The child I gave the money to bowed to me in thanks several times and walked into the middle of the field where the other boys attacked him and took the money. Now he was not only hungry but had suffered a beating as well. I wanted to do something but was urged not to interfere. Some of the staff from MacDonald's chased away any of the urchins who got too close to their customers. To most of the Turks, the children were invisible.

I say all this to set the stage for what happened later. This wonderful Turkish woman lived a life that had a set of parameters that she did not violate. Within those rules she always felt safe. To us many of those rules were harsh and restrictive. She knew her place within those rules and felt safe in that environment. Remember that she is a college educated woman who had worked with Americans every day for several years.

One of the ways we Americans would show our thanks to our best Turkish employees involved the "training reward." Most Turks have never been out of Turkey and probably never would be. As members of the Services Squadron, Turkish employees could be sent to San Antonio, Texas for training. This was viewed as the ultimate compliment that we could pay an employee. About six months after I returned to the United States, this young lady was rewarded with a training trip to San Antonio. One night my telephone range and to my surprise, it was this young lady. She was sobbing and near hysteria. She was alone in America, without any family or friends, attending the Services Squadron training. She went to her hotel and checked in. As she walked to her room, she passed a room with an open door. Inside the room there was a man sitting on his bed in his underwear. She was terrified by the sight. After I got her calmed down enough to understand her, it became apparent to me that the mere sight of a nearly naked man was totally un-nerving to her. She didn't know what his intentions were. Would he try to attack her? Why would he sit there like that with his door open? Having no real feel for the size of America, she asked if I would come and protect her. How long would it take for me to get there? When I told her that I was too far away, she wanted go home immediately. She actually cut her trip to America short so that she could get home and feel safe again.

Do you think she wants Turkey to turn into a copy of America? I doubt it. If a well educated, non-Moslem, female who worked with Americans on a daily basis for years wanted no part of America then how do you expect the average un-educated mid-easterner to accept us without reservation. The rest of the world may want to copy certain aspects of America but they do not want to be a carbon copy of our society. Most American's can't understand this. They are totally blind to the fact that one size does not fit all. Our form of government doesn't really work that well for us anymore and yet we want to force other countries to accept it for their own.

It was only a few years ago that we didn't care what your government was as long as it was anti-communist. Those were the good old days. We supported the Shah of Iran for more than twenty five years because he was anti-communist and his reign helped stabilize the mid-east. We didn't care that he was a dictator. He was our dictator.

We supported Noriega in South America as well as many other anti-communist dictators. When the Imam's assumed power in Iran and became anti-American, we supported a new guy in Iraq, Saddam Hussein. This was to counter-balance Iran's influence in the area. We had to spank him when he invaded Kuwait but he thought that since we supported his takeover of Iraq, we would ignore what he did within his own borders. When we simply chased his forces out of Kuwait and then didn't finish the job of deposing him, he was sure of our intentions.

Imagine his surprise when some terrorists from Saudi Arabia attacked America and we started kicking his butt in response. It wasn't just Saddam Hussein who was baffled by our behavior. It was the whole Arab world. First we go one way, then the other, all the while acting as if we are doing the world a favor by our every action.

CHAPTER THIRTY

Politics

When I was in High School, abortion was illegal almost everywhere. There was always some shady, back alley clinic that practiced illegal abortions. You would literally take your life in your hands when you went to one. The clinics were often un-sanitary and many of the support staff were poorly trained. The procedure was accomplished in a hurry to make the chance of getting caught a lot smaller and so that they could make more money by seeing more patients. Many of the people actually performing the abortions were also poorly trained and aftercare was practically non-existent.

Someone I knew got pregnant and then caught the "New York flu." That's what they called a trip to New York City for an abortion in those days. A girl got pregnant. She disappeared for a few days. When she reappeared, she was not pregnant and she had just come from a wonderful trip to New York where she caught the flu. The flu was the explanation for why the girl looked pale and withdrawn for a few days.

Abortion was one of the top debate subjects in competitions all over America. Women proclaimed that it was their body and they should have the right to decide. That was years before the "Pro Choice" slogan was developed. That was also before the far right decided that a fetus should have the full rights of a human beginning when your father picked up your mother for the date on which you were conceived. Yes, I am exaggerating a little but not much. Take a look at the recent vote in Mississippi that wanted to grant "personhood" the instant the sperm attached itself to the egg. The fallout from this would have ended *Roe v Wade* and could even have allowed prosecution for mothers who had a miscarriage (criminal negligence). Thankfully, it was not passed in Mississippi, but some fringe groups are trying to get it passed in other states. The good thing about this attempt was that they at least allowed the people to vote on it. We are a democracy so the rule of the majority should be the law of the land.

Both the liberals and the conservatives have tried to have it their way by stacking the courts with people that think like they do. Each time there is a new president, he tries to get as many judges appointed from his team as possible. Since this is a democracy you would think it a simple task to put abortion to a national vote and let the people decide. The dirty little secret is that neither side wants that because they are afraid they might lose. Another reason for them to keep the issue alive is the fund raising potential for both sides when they carry on the fight. No one can raise money on the issue once it has been decided.

It used to be a lot simpler. Either you wanted the woman to have a choice of what to do with her own body or you didn't. Now the conservatives want to stop the spending of tax dollars to pay for abortions. They want to stop teaching birth control in health class at school. They deny the reality that many women simply cannot afford to raise a child right now. Their smug, self righteous answer is that they shouldn't have had sex then. It's similar to their chant about criminals. They should have considered the consequences before they broke the law. Most of the time there is very little thinking going on when in the throes of passion.

When we are young we are driven by nature to breed. There is a time in every young person's life when hormones are close to driving them insane! If not insane, then at the very least, they lose control of their sexual desires and definitely are not thinking about the possible consequences. That is why the fundamentalist doctrine of abstinence is such a farce. There are even those on the far right that want to withhold federal money from schools if the school teaches anything other than abstinence in health class. It used to be called "sex education" but that is not PC anymore. Ignorance of cause and effect should never be the answer. Pretending like a problem doesn't exist will not make it go away.

Almost every day another poll is released indicating that most Americans think that politicians are corrupt, liars, and self indulgent pendejos. In spite of this they re-elect the same people year after year. Do they consider the pendejo they know to be superior to the pendejo they don't know? My observation on this is that people believe what they want to believe. The truth has no part in it.

Years ago I worked at a state run delinquent youth center. They had an inmate council and it was election time for the council president. There was one candidate who played by the rules and was actually an all round straight shooter. It made you wonder how he got in a jam and ended up there in the first place. He campaigned on issues that he knew he could have some control over. Things that would make life for the inmates better. His opponent ran on the popular platform of "blue jeans and pussy on Sundays." He won by a landslide.

No one ever stopped to think that the president of the inmate council had no chance of changing the rules to allow the wear of blue jeans or the establishment of conjugal visits every Sunday. They just voted for the person who told them what they wanted to hear. In my experience that example translates to America as a whole.

People listen to what they want to hear and believe only what they want to believe. Logic or factual basis has nothing to do with it. When a Presidential candidate tells us about all the changes he will make if you will only vote for him, you should just run away screaming and pulling your hair. Because of our system of checks and balances, no President can change much of anything without the support of the House and the Senate. He can ask them to change things. He can make suggestions. He can even work behind the scenes to garner support for changes in legislation but he cannot arbitrarily make changes. When other politicians claim that they will change the sun, moon and stars so that they line up according to your wishes, they are also straying from the truth. People want to believe in the "magic bullet." They want to believe that one politician can change everything because they say they can. It's just not true.

Sometimes accidents happen and a bizarre twist of fate will change history. In Alabama there had been no Republican governor elected since the Yankee imposed Reconstruction but that was about to change.

For more than a century the Democratic primary was the de facto general election. The Republicans would run a slate of candidates just to give the appearance of a two party system. There was a nut job candidate for the Democratic nomination named Charlie Graddick. He had been the State Attorney General and his campaign was straight out of the Old

Testament. His TV commercial featured him slamming a jail cell door and claiming he would lock up all criminals. All the God fearing, Old Testament, King James Version of the Bible believing types immediately took him into their hearts and gave him their votes. The state Democratic Party insiders didn't want him to be governor. They wanted Bill Baxley, Alabama's Lieutenant Governor and a member of the party elite. The Democratic primary was indecisive. In the resulting runoff election on June 24, Attorney General Charlie Graddick narrowly defeated Lieutenant Governor Bill Baxley. Graddick, the state's chief law enforcement officer, was then accused in a federal court suit of having encouraged and allowed Republicans to vote in the Democratic primary. This action diluted the votes of black voters and violated the provisions of the 1965 Voting Rights Act. They then named Bill Baxley as the Democratic Party candidate. The people of the state were irate. When Party leaders gave the nomination to Baxley, it created a furor among Alabama voters, who believed they had been stripped of their power to elect their governor of choice.

For years the Republicans had fielded a slate of perennial losers just so there appeared to be some competition for state offices. One of the perennial losers was Guy Hunt. He was a primitive Baptist preacher from a small town in north Alabama called Holly Pond.

Charlie Graddick originally threatened to wage a write-in campaign but then changed his mind. Guy Hunt, who was originally viewed as the Republican's sacrificial lamb, saw his chances greatly improve with Graddick out of the race.

Bill Baxley ridiculed Hunt as unqualified because he had not attended college and worked as an Amway products distributor and chicken farmer in addition to being a part-time

203

Primitive Baptist preacher. A rumor floated that Hunt was asked to leave his federal job because he had solicited campaign contributions from his employees. Hunt stressed economic development issues and courted conservative Democrats. He benefited from what the public perceived as "dirty Democratic" politics and was elected by a decisive fifty six percent to forty four percent margin on November 4, 1986. He was the first Republican to hold this office since David Peter Lewis in 1872. He was also the first to be removed from that office following his 1993 conviction on ethics charges.

The people of Alabama didn't really vote for Guy Hunt but they voted against Bill Baxley and dirty Democratic politics. Once Guy Hunt was Governor, the Republican Party experienced a rebirth in Alabama. It was no longer considered a joke to be a registered Republican. As time passed, Alabama has become a Democratic state on the local level and a Republican state on the statewide level. Every candidate tries to convince the voters that they are more conservative than the people they are running against. I used to say that an Alabama Democrat would be a Republican anywhere else. To be more conservative than an Alabama Democrat you would probably have to be a Nazi. Then the earth shifted on its axis and the whole state went Republican.

If you ask an Alabama politician why they left the Democratic Party they will say they didn't leave it, the Democratic Party left them. That's their way of saying that the pointy headed intellectuals and liberals took over the Democratic Party. Sounds much like the Democrats saying that the modern Tea Party has taken over the Republican Party. It's a generalization that the majority of the people believe. Adolf Hitler said that people have trouble believing little lies but they will always believe the big lie. He also perfected the art of saying a thing over and over until it literally became the truth. At least it was perceived to be the truth and that's really all that matters. Politicians are trained today by their professional handlers to do just that. They are trained to speak in sound bites and to repeat those sound bites over and over until they become the truth in people's minds. Apparently it is a very effective campaign technique.

On the other hand, the national spotlight that is shone on candidates today precludes the best and brightest from ever being elected to higher office. Some of the most valuable lessons I've ever learned were learned because I made a mistake. In the political world, its one mistake and you are eliminated from contention. God forbid that you have made more than one mistake in your life. If you have and the mistakes are discovered, then you will be labeled a scumbag loser and banished from the sight of decent humans. You may have learned from your mistakes and become the best human being that you can be today and it doesn't matter.

It's a lot like the way the Navy promotes its Officers. The Officer Corps is an upside down pyramid with fewer positions available the higher you go. Since it is so competitive and they all start with the same basic qualifications, it becomes a matter of finding the disqualifiers to weed out the less than perfect candidates for promotion. They spend more time looking for reasons not to promote than for reason that a person should be promoted. That is probably because it is easier to defend a disqualification than it is to prove how good a leader someone is when all the fitness reports are inflated to begin with.

The absolute best Navy Officer I ever worked with was a Captain who would never be considered for promotion to

Admiral because of something one of his Junior Officers did while he was in a Command position. That "disqualifier" deprived America of one of the best leaders I've seen in the Navy. You have all heard that not all pigs are created equal or that some pigs are more equal than others. He was definitely more equal than the others.

I attended a meeting in Washington, DC that included more than a dozen Navy Captains representing numerous specialties within the Navy. They were all talking over each other and getting nowhere. This Captain walked in and stood there a moment quietly assessing the situation. He then walked to the blackboard and began to write an outline. A hush came over the room. When he was finished he turned to the group and began to speak. The whole room listened attentively. In minutes he had taken charge of the situation and provided leadership to the roomful of Captains. It was his natural leadership ability and command presence that made everyone fall into line. If there has ever been Admiral material then this man represented a shining example. He was made to retire as a Captain leaving a leadership void that still has not been filled.

Until America demands that the best and brightest are promoted and allowed to lead the country then we are doomed to be second rate. There is no place in a free market, capitalism based society for set asides and programs designed to make up for the sins of our ancestors.

Much is written bewailing the fact that we are slipping from our position of preeminence in the world. Writers pontificate about the various PC reasons that might cause the situation. They insist that various groups suffer from a lack of opportunity. They say that if we would only give them preferential treatment to make up for past abuses, then all will be well. The real answer is the one right in front of their face.

We have deviated from the laws of nature and we are paying the price. We can't evolve to a higher level of homo-sapiens when we continue to reward mediocrity. In the case of today's military promotions, it is more important not to ever do anything wrong than it is to be a great leader. That stifles creativity and develops a group of corporate "yes men" who will eventually make it to the top.

I personally witnessed as far back as the 80's (but it probably existed further back than that) that Army leadership was famous for never wanting to make a decision. They would get together a group of Officers and come to a consensus. Once the group made a recommendation, the Officer in charge would always go along with the group choice. That way, if the decision was the wrong one, the leader could deny responsibility because his staff gave him the wrong information.

A favorite tactic of these group decisions was to try to anticipate what the boss wanted and make a recommendation that supported what you think the boss wants. You can see the problems with this approach. The truth doesn't enter in to the equation. Facts mean nothing. Only the desire to be seen as supportive of the leader's preconceived notion is important. If you present facts that are at odds with your military leader then you are seen as being misinformed at best and obstructionist or obstinate at worst. If you receive either identifier you are cast in a bad light and probably just earned that disqualifier keeping you from higher promotions that I mentioned earlier.

Sometimes you get a military boss who thinks he is a world changer. He comes in with a preconceived notion that everything and everybody is screwed up and only he can make it right. I served under one of these world changers while working for Navy advertising. My job was to manage the national advertising program for one of the recruiting segments. My new officer/boss had an idea that the annual planner/calendar that had been produced for more than twenty years should be replaced by a mouse pad calendar. I must point out that the reason the original product was a planner is that by law, the Navy can't produce and print a calendar so they publish a desktop planner that just happens to contain a calendar. That apparently makes it legal to print using government money. They usually spent about $350,000 a year printing these planners.

The recruiters waited expectantly for them each year. They used them as a ticket to get into the local schools. The desk sized planners were very popular among the teachers and guidance counselors because they contained information about scholarship offers, SAT testing dates, and had plenty of room for the teacher's notes. Several years ago, another "world changing" officer came in who tried to kill the planner. That officer almost lost his job over the complaints coming from the field recruiters. He was ordered to get it printed and into the hands of the field recruiters ASAP.

Roll the clock forward a few years. The new "World Changing" Officer in Charge was convinced that he knew everything and the employees just wanted to maintain the status quo because they were lazy and obstinate. All the professional members of his staff told him that the recruiters would eat his lunch if he did away with their planner. He actually insisted that his wife thought it was a good idea so all who opposed must be wrong. He gave the order that the desktop planner was out and the mouse pad calendar was in. He was sure everyone would love it.

As you may have guessed, the mouse pad calendar was a dismal failure. For one thing, no one uses a mouse pad any more. There was also no room for the teacher's notes. The final factor was the mouse pad was really cheesy and cheap looking. Of course he never apologized to anyone who tried to keep him out of trouble. Instead, he holds a grudge against them. He actually believed that if only the mouse pad had a non slip back on it like he wanted, then the recruiters would have loved it. The moral of this story is that any boss should look to the experts that have institutional memory and years of experience for advice and then they should follow it. Why have experts on your team if you don't plan to listen to them?

The aliens agreed with me that this is a universal problem and not limited to humans. They then asked me some specific questions related to our earlier discussions. One of the questions they asked was in response to the statement that sometimes humans will plead guilty to something that they know they didn't do. How could this be they asked? A lot of humans have asked this question. You have to have some experience with the American Justice system to understand the answer.

Every American is entitled to their day in court. They are entitled to know what they are being charged with and to be judged by a jury of their peers. Therein lays the rub. Who is to say who your peers are? If you are a genius, do they convene a jury made up of people with a genius IQ? If you are male will it be an all male jury? Will your jury remotely resemble you? The answer is an emphatic no. Both the prosecution and the defense will try to load the jury with those people that they feel will be sympathetic to their position. They are most assuredly not your peers. It's all up to how they feel that day as to how they will vote. Because of the chance that the prosecution will be believed over the defense, many people will "take the deal."

As mentioned before, prosecutors are judged by their conviction rate. They will settle most cases with a plea bargain. That means they will offer to convict you of a lesser charge if you will plead guilty. This guarantees them another conviction for their record.

A key consideration for the defendant in accepting the offer of a plea bargain for a lesser charge is this: How much justice can you afford? If it costs five thousand dollars to get a lawyer to defend you on a charge and the District Attorney offers to let you plead guilty to a lesser charge which calls for a fine of one hundred dollars plus court cost, you will most likely plead guilty. Even if you win the original court case and are found innocent, the State is not liable to pay you back for your legal expenses. You will be out five thousand dollars instead of a one hundred dollar fine plus court cost. There have been many cases where the District Attorney knows he can't get a conviction but he takes the case to court anyway. He knows that he can still punish you by making you spend money on legal fees. They often use this tactic when dealing with organized crime, drug dealers, or any other person or group that they wish to target.

There is another questionable situation I have witnessed concerning plea bargaining. This involves the "back room deal". When a socially prominent individual is arrested, his lawyer may offer to get a less prominent individual to plead guilty to a significant charge, and trade this plea for a reduced charge for the prominent individual. Of course, the less

210

prominent person is not aware that this deal ever takes place. In fact, the lawyer will try to scare the poor client into a plea deal, all the time knowing it is not right or ethical. It's a simple dollars and cents move. They can make more money for getting the prominent person off the hook than they can for the poor client.

The other aspect of "all the justice you can afford" results from your ability to pay a good lawyer to defend you versus the indigent who must make do with a court appointed lawyer. Your court appointed lawyer will often use you as a bargaining chip to help a better paying customer get off. Even among lawyers you pay, there are various ranges of competency. You read every day about the errors that some lawyers commit or see being committed in a case yet do nothing about them.

If you can afford a good lawyer and you can afford to spend what it takes to win, you have a good chance of getting off, even if guilty. Think of the first O.J. Simpson case. Most people believe that he got away with murder but his high priced legal team was able to out talk the prosecution. If you don't have the means then you stand a good chance of going to jail even if innocent. Many people will say that innocent people have nothing to worry about. Even if not convicted, financial ruin is a very real possibility if you are ever charged with a serious crime.

The aliens asked me how this could be. Didn't the lawyers swear to "seek out the truth, the whole truth, and nothing but the truth?" In a race where telepathy is the norm, the concept of telling a lie is hard to understand.

CHAPTER THIRTY-ONE

Too Many People

It seems like everything that we talked about supported the aliens idea that it might be time for a do over. As a member of the human race I was trying my best to think of reasons to give us another chance to straighten things out. I asked the leader of the aliens if there was any reason why they had to rush to judgment or could they give us another couple of hundred years to get things right. They immediately told me about the booming population on earth today and where it is projected to be in the near future. From my living room at my home out in the country, it looks like there is plenty of room for more people. The aliens agreed with me that there is plenty of room for the actual people but there is not enough room to grow the food required to feed them. They also pointed out that too many of the earth's people are living in the wrong places.

The human population of earth grew pretty slowly at first. When we were hunter/gatherers the lack of food kept the population down. As we developed agriculture, the human population grew more rapidly. It still took until about 1810 for the earth's human population to reach one billion. By 1900 it had grown to about one point six billion. Around this time, the use of petroleum products became common. This allowed more efficient machines to be developed to assist in agricultural efforts. Not only could more food be grown, but food could be transported farther from the source than ever before. This caused the population to explode. By 1970 the population more than doubled to about three point seven billion. By 2011 it reached seven billion people. Conservative estimates say it will reach ten point five billion by 2050. The natural resources of earth cannot support a continuous expansion of the human population. There is not enough arable land, clean water resources, and oil left to support an infinite number of humans. Back in 1978 there was an estimate published that said all the earth's oil would be used up in sixty to ninety years. According to a *Time Magazine* story published in October 1978, the source of that "sixty to ninety year" figure was an official report produced for the Central Intelligence Agency.

Once the oil runs out, how will the huge farms be operated? How will the food get moved from point of production to area of need? A lot of fertilizer and pesticides are petroleum based. When the bugs can't be controlled, the yields will drop.

We have huge areas of the world today where the people are starving and don't have clean water to drink. The under developed parts of the world are where the highest birth rates are. Many of the more advanced countries are actually seeing a decline in the birth rate. This means that those who are least able to sustain a growing population are the very ones having the most children. It was recently reported in the news that Catholic Bishops in India were encouraging their parishioners to have more babies because the percentage of Christians in India was decreasing. How can anyone in good conscience recommend that more babies be brought into the world in the

213

second most populous nation on earth? India has millions of people living in abject poverty and the Catholic Church wants them to increase the number of Catholic babies so their percent of market share will grow! This is another example of religion running amok.

Images of mobs of people rioting and burning and pillaging appeared in my head. Millions of starving people with nothing to lose will be swarming out of the infertile, dry areas of the earth looking for anything to eat or drink.

With the oil deposits of the earth dissipated, what will the world use for transportation? Can the whole world change to electric cars or steam powered cars or some other undiscovered technology in time to stave off an epic collapse of society? Since we have known for more than thirty years that the oil is running out, shouldn't we be much further along in making the required shift to new technologies? The answer from the alien leader was a resounding "yes." The people of earth keep breeding more people into a system that cannot feed them all at current levels. How bad will it be by 2050 or 2100, or even later if this trend continues?

One of the scariest problems we face is the lack of clear, clean, drinkable water. This shortage could actually cause a lot of problems even before the lack of oil causes widespread starvation. For years we have ruthlessly polluted the earth's water. We have irrigated vast areas of desert, using water as if there is an unlimited supply. Man has dammed rivers, diverting the flow of fresh water from its natural destination, the sea. About thirty years ago, several rivers were diverted from flowing into the Aral Sea. Today, the Aral Sea is half as large as it was and the waters are three times as salty as before. All species of fish that used to live in the Aral Sea have died off.

214

The river water was diverted with no thought of the unintended consequences.

In the United States the average person acts as if water will always be available. We use more water per person than any country on the planet. In fact there are areas of America where we face catastrophic water shortages now. Many of the reservoirs in the Southwest have totally dried up. A lot of the others are facing the lowest water levels in memory. Because of the immense concentration of population around the larger cities, it is very difficult to keep them supplied with potable water. The resort city of Las Vegas is living on borrowed time unless something is done soon. It is hard to imagine but we simultaneously have record flooding and record drought conditions in this country. If only we had invested in the infrastructure to pipe water from flood prone areas to the dry areas. I guess that pipelines to move water around America aren't sexy enough to attract the attention of our politicians.

What happens to a mid-eastern country with little water, whose oil is running out, and is filled with people who are hungry but have invested in nuclear weapons? With nothing to lose will they start a thermo nuclear war that will devastate the earth? Why not? They have nothing to lose when they face starvation, death from lack of water, and an end to the flow of riches created by the oil deposits under their country.

The picture painted by the alien leader is bleak. Do we let the humans overpopulate to the point where they use up all the oil, contaminate the soil and water, foul the very air that we breath to a point where it too is unusable? I was beginning to believe that the alien's idea of a do over might be more humane than letting nature take its course. Unless something significant changes in the way humans interact with each other and with

215

the planet on which they live, the final outcome is guaranteed. The big question is how many other species do we take down with us?

It seems like every day you read about another species becoming extinct or at least added to the endangered list. I'm not just talking about tiny fish like the snail darter or some obscure type of butterfly either. Think about the Passenger Pigeon. When North America was first settled, there were so many Passenger Pigeons that the sky would be dark as their vast flocks migrated across the country. By 1914, the last Passenger Pigeon died in a zoo. They were hunted for cheap food and killed for sport until none were left. The Dodo bird met a similar fate. It was first seen by Europeans in 1507 and was extinct by 1681. Not only was it killed for food, a host of new predators were introduced that helped seal their fate. I recently read that the Bengal Tiger population in the wild had fallen to around twenty five hundred. There are more of them in zoos around the world than in the wild. I could go on listing species that have suffered at the hands of the human race but you get the picture.

Any time the choice is go hungry or eat anything that moves, humans choose to eat anything that moves. That includes each other. There have been whole societies within the human population that practiced cannibalism even when times were good. When times are bad, even so called civilized people have chosen cannibalism over starvation. Think about the infamous Donner Party that got caught in the snowy mountain pass and only survived by resorting to eating the dead. In 1972 there was a soccer team that crashed in the Andes. After a search was called off, they were all listed as dead. This resulted in the sixteen survivors living for around two months by eating the remains of the other victims of the crash. Both these events show how regular people can respond to starvation.

In many other societies, they are not that far away from ancestors who routinely ate the flesh of other humans. Sometimes it was simply for food and sometimes it was for religious reasons. When the primary source of available protein is the human standing next to you, how long before your survival instincts take over? When will natures law of survival of the fittest take over from the artificial rules that the human race has wrapped itself in? These are legitimate questions that I don't really want to contemplate, much less answer.

CHAPTER THIRTY-TWO

What Can We Do?

All the things the aliens told me began to weigh down my spirits to the point that it seemed the only thing to do was give up. It seems that everywhere you look, people only think of themselves and their immediate wants and needs. They don't seem capable of postponing instant gratification in support of achieving a long term goal. We need to return to a way of life kind of like the national ethic that used to govern the behavior of most Americans. People planned ahead and saved up their money to buy things. They didn't have to have it all right now. Families worked together to get better education for their children so their opportunities to live the good life would be improved from one generation to the next. Can we do it? Can we change our ways and get back to a lifestyle more in tune with the laws of nature? What specific things can we do to make America better quickly and in the long run, serve as the good example and guiding light for the rest of the world as we did in the not so distant past?

The leader of the aliens said: "When you begin to understand where your people came from and what got you into the current situation, only then will you be able to map a path to a viable future."

"That sounds like something I've read on a fortune cookie at my favorite Chinese Buffet. Give me some concrete examples of what we should do to turn this thing around."

The alien responded: "You must immediately begin to live as one with nature. This means that the laws of natural selection and survival of the fittest must be embraced." He then began to outline a plan for the continued viability of mankind.

Much has been written, discussed and legislated in America concerning the equality of man. In general it is said that all men are created equal. Nothing could be further from the truth.

In America, all people are created with the equal opportunity to achieve as much as their natural abilities allow. They are guaranteed a chance. They are not guaranteed success. It is absolutely absurd to believe that we are all equal.

Some people are smarter than others. Some people are taller, faster, stronger, or better looking than others. Some people are born to rich families and some are born to poor families. Current thinking seems to be that since we can't raise up the low, we will restrict the success of the high. We will artificially hold back the high achievers by giving opportunities they deserve, based on ability, to those with less ability. We must stop this at once. The best person for the job, regardless of race, sex, color, age, or creed is who should get it. No other factors should be considered.

The same goes for scholarship programs. Everyone should not aspire to college graduation. There is nothing wrong with being happy doing a job that does not require a college degree. We have artificially inflated expectations to the point where we feel that we are "settling" when we don't get that degree. The world needs craftsmen, laborers, farmers, truck drivers, mechanics, and so on. They are not failures unless they are clearly able to do more and simply choose to do less because they are lazy.

Society does not owe success to anyone. Society should reward excellence and discourage mediocrity. We do this in sports and no one says a word. Imagine a scrawny, slow, short, white guy with no vertical leap, suing the NBA because he wasn't selected to play basketball. He clearly is non-competitive but if you use the logic applied to other set aside programs, it would be perfectly logical for this person to expect special consideration based on his groups years of suffering from not playing in the NBA. I can hear the howls of outrage at this comparison but at the end of the day, a job is a job, is a job. Where do you draw the line?

The Navy desperately needs Doctors so they have established a scholarship program to pay the full cost of a medical school education plus a stipend and a nice sign on bonus. Enter the PC Police. Since quotas have been determined to be bad, "goals" have replaced them. Goals are good. Quotas are bad. The PC Police dictate that there should be a goal for minority students within the program.

In order to achieve that goal, lower achieving minority students are brought into the program, keeping higher performing students from receiving the scholarships. I was told by someone who should know, that the dropout rate of one segment of the minority students is about nine times the dropout rate of the general population. The result is that the Navy has wasted a lot of time and money in the name of political correctness AND ended up without the services of a number of doctors that they really needed.

I go back to the Constitution and its implied promise of equal opportunity based on your ability. There is no guarantee of success either expressed or implied. What happened to the right of equal opportunity that should have been offered to the higher achieving medical students? They actually had their rights violated in the name of political correctness. Where is the outrage? This must be changed at once if we are to return to greatness.

A reality check should take place immediately. We must understand that though Democracy is an integral part of the American way of life, it is not for everyone. If a country does not bother us, then what they do within their borders is of no concern to us. When we support a government because they are an enemy of our enemy, then we should support them no matter what. We should not try to dictate how they will treat their people or what form of government they should have. Most of the world just wants something to eat, to be safe, and know what the rules are so they can get on with living. What their government does is so abstract to them as to not matter.

Our enemy of the day seems to be Iran. For years the Shah of Iran was our friend. It was all because he was against the communists. We turned our back on him and the Mideast has been in turmoil ever since. We attempted to develop a new balancing act in the region when we supported a new dictator, Saddam Hussein of Iraq. Imagine how he felt after we spanked him during Desert Storm, flew Operation Northern Watch and Operation Southern Watch for about ten years (this destroyed his Air Force and maintained a foreign aviation presence over his sovereign nation the whole time) and then invaded his country and eventually destroyed both the country and him personally.

We have to understand that if we support a country's government, then we have to be true to that pledge of support unless they attack us. We can't switch because of a change in the political environment of this country. Just because a different political party controls the White House, it is not justification for us to abandon old allies and switch to new ones. We have to maintain our integrity over the long term. The PC police must stay out of our foreign affairs.

So much of our time and money has been spent on trying to convert the rest of the planet into copies of America that we have allowed our own country to get terribly dilapidated. Roads, railroads, bridges, pipelines to shift water resources to where they are critically needed are all in need of immediate action. That's just the tip of the iceberg. We used to invest in innovation, education, and continual improvement of the American way of life. We have to get back to that. When we return to that plan of action, we will regain our place as a world leader in all things. All our people who want them will have jobs in the revitalization of America. National pride will lead to greater innovation. The downward spiral we are currently in will reverse itself totally.

We have to reinvest in the infrastructure of our nation instead of spending our money nation building on the other side of the planet. If we built a pipeline to move water from the Mississippi River to the plains of Texas and points further west, we could control flooding all along the Ohio and Mississippi River basins and relieve drought conditions at the same time. It would also provide employment for thousands of people. Our roads are in sad shape. Bridges are becoming unsafe. Do we have to wait till they collapse to realize that they won't last forever? Reinvestment in the infrastructure is an investment in jobs. More jobs mean more tax payers. More tax payers mean we can pay down the deficit without raising taxes. The concept is so simple that it evades most people. It's a simple rule of business.

Cut costs where you can and increase revenue. You can increase revenue the old fashioned way by removing obstacles to earning. You can fashion a better product. You can incentivize productivity instead of trying to suppress it. We must level the playing field by making everyone share the load.

This does not mean we should redistribute the wealth as the current political regime is determined to do. In nature, the Alpha dog gets the best of everything because he is the Alpha dog. Nature gives every creature the opportunity to grow into the Alpha member of its group. The limiting factor is genetic. Some animals just don't have the same qualities as others. You must remember that humans are just another animal residing on the planet earth.

We must immediately begin a cultural change from the gas guzzling muscle cars and trucks that we seem to be addicted to. The technology exists today to make fuel efficient vehicles but no one really wants them. Most people still want lots of power and the comfort of a large and heavy car. How far do most people drive at one time? Do they really need a land yacht just to drive 10 miles to work? A lot of people try to justify their large autos by saying they are safer than the smaller cars. If they are safer for you, and that is a disputable point, then their size makes them less safe for those you run into. Why have a vehicle that is capable of running over one hundred miles per hour when there is no road in America where it is legal to travel that fast?

More investment must be made into sustainable and renewable energy sources. Bio-fuels do not have to be made from products we normally eat. Corn is not the only agricultural product available to convert to alcohol for ethanol. Sugarcane and switch grass are both easy to use in making alcohol and are actually much more efficient than corn. Brazil is now totally energy independent because they require cars to be flex fuel equipped. Most cars can run on any combination of gasoline and alcohol. Some of them can run on one hundred percent alcohol. They actually have between two and three million cars on the road equipped to operate on one hundred percent alcohol. By August of 2009, ninety four percent of the cars sold there were flex cars.

They eat their corn so they use mostly sugarcane to produce the alcohol. Recent research has determined that algae can be used to create bio-fuel. It is forty percent cheaper to produce this way and one hundred to three hundred times more oil per acre can be produced than with other agricultural products. We have to embrace more reasonable cars that are designed to do what we need instead of what we want. The alternative is to cling to the dinosaurs Detroit has produced in the past and run completely out of oil in the next few decades. We can't afford to wait till the oil is gone to make the switch. We must stretch available resources as much as we can instead of continuing to deplete them at a break neck pace.

People have to understand that success requires effort. You must be willing to give something to get something. I was too poor to go to college but I gave four years of my life to military service so that I could earn the GI Bill. I used the GI Bill to earn three degrees, including a Master of Science. If you look for it, there is a workable solution to almost every problem we face. Quitters never win and winners never quit. It sounds trite but it is true.

No one owes you any and everything just because you happen to be alive. Participation trophies are out and awards for success are back in style. We will still applaud your efforts for trying but you will not be pampered to the point that the smallest set back leaves you wondering, "What's the other guy's problem?" After all, the current generation has always been told how special each and every one of them is. There are no losers. Everyone is a winner! Societal pressure and the PC police have created unrealistic expectations and we must go back to the natural competitiveness of nature. Natural selection and survival of the fittest should be the law of the land, if we want to prosper again.

We also must adjust our thinking in the area of the military. We can't go on paying so much money for defense just so they can have all the toys they want. The Union of Soviet Socialist Republics, or Soviet Union, went broke trying to maintain a military machine that used up too much of their gross national product. When they went broke, the Union dissolved and went back to being a group of third world countries. We must return to the days when military service was considered a service to the nation. The modern military has one of the best propaganda machines in the world trying to convince the general population how hard it is to be in the military. The facts are far different. Through guilt, based on memories of abuses that occurred during the Draft years, we have gold plated military service.

An independent group looked at military compensation and found that it is about thirty five percent higher than civilian jobs doing similar tasks. The retirement program is incredibly generous and then you add on the modern GI Bill. It pays one hundred percent tuition and gives you an allowance to live on while in school. If you don't use it, you can give it to your children to use.

Every conceivable service is provided military families to include tax free shopping, low cost groceries subsidized by government dollars, gyms, fitness centers, sports programs, child care centers and more. Our promise to service members is that we provide similar services that one could expect in their local communities. What we actually provide is so much better than most local communities have that it borders on criminal.

The proof of this rhetoric is that retention is at an all time high in all the military services. They do not want to get out. Most of them don't retire with twenty year's service. They won't retire until they are made to leave. They then expect to be given preference for a government job – but want to start at the top. They feel entitled to special treatment since they suffered through a high paying, gold plated existence for so many years.

I realize that many of our actual combat soldiers have paid the ultimate price and lost life or limbs but this is a small proportion of the people in service. It takes between seven and twelve support troops to field one combat soldier. Most service members never hear a shot fired in anger yet believe they should receive cradle to grave special treatment. We need a reality check here. What we have been doing is unsustainable and is not in the best interest of this country.

There was a time in this country when members of Congress and Senators were looked up to. They were successful members of society that were interested in making America better. They made a great personal sacrifice to serve this country. Even when they didn't agree, they found some way to move America forward.

Self interest seems to be the modus operandi of America's so called leadership today. Once they get in power it's the backroom deals with lobbyists that trump the needs of the people. It's the desire to win for their Party at the detriment of the opposition that motivates their votes instead of creating a consensus that both sides can live with.

A great salesman taught me that the best sales are those that leave both sides feeling like they won. There should not be a winner and a loser every time. The vision and dream that is America is all that is important. Party politics and self promotion should be banished from the process. All the way up to the Presidency they seem to be campaigning for re-election year round instead of doing what is best for America. This must stop immediately.

To paraphrase Einstein, "It's pure insanity to continue to do the same things and expect a different outcome." That's what we are doing today and that is what must be changed if we want to continue to exist as the beacon of freedom and opportunity that we used to represent.

After the alien leader told me all that, I just shook my head in dismay. The solutions are simple yet they require fundamental changes in the way Americans do things today. Have we all become so selfish and self indulgent that the future is hopeless?

As I stood there trying to decide whether the aliens would or even should give us another chance, there was a bright flash of light. I temporarily blacked out. When I came to my senses I was sitting on my Harley in the middle of that lonely stretch of road. I shook my head to clear the cobwebs, looked to the left and right, then up in the sky overhead. I didn't see anything so I cranked my bike and tore out of there.

At first I wondered if it was all a dream. Then I looked at myself in the mirror and realized that it really happened. I was taller than before, stronger, totally pain free, and my mind was filled with information that I didn't have before my time spent with the aliens. The ultimate proof was that I now appeared to be at least thirty years younger!

When I look back on this whole experience it makes me wonder how much of what the aliens said is true. Have humans been as bad as they made out? If you believe half of the stories they told me then you have to admit that we have treated the planet and each other very badly. I'm going to spend a lot of time on Google and in the library looking up information to prove or disprove the alien's tales. If they told the truth then I will spend the rest of my life trying to spread the word and get humanity back on the right track.

Although I am only one person, I'll pass on the stories and try to get my fellow humans to realize the error of their ways. With my alien enhanced abilities maybe I can get people to listen and to begin to think for themselves instead of blindly following the herd.

It is also possible that the aliens may have adjusted others. If they exist, I will do my best to seek them out. If we pool our alien augmented talents just maybe we can make a difference. Maybe it's not too late and the aliens will give us one more chance.

The question we must ask: Is this the end or the beginning?